From Dylan to Donne
BRIDGING ENGLISH AND MUSIC

Brock Dethier

Boynton/Cook Publishers
HEINEMANN
Portsmouth, NH

Boynton/Cook Publishers, Inc.
A subsidiary of Reed Elsevier Inc.
361 Hanover Street
Portsmouth, NH 03801–3912
www.boyntoncook.com

Offices and agents throughout the world

The author and publisher wish to thank those who have generously given permission to reprint borrowed material:

Excerpts from *It's Not Only Rock & Roll* by Peter Christenson and Donald Roberts. Copyright © 1998. Published by Hampton Press. Reprinted by permission of the publisher.

Lyrics from "Not a Pretty Girl" by Ani DiFranco. Copyright © 1995 by Righteous Babe Music. All rights reserved. Used by permission.

Lyrics from "Gloria" by Van Morrison. Reprinted by permission of Bernice Music Inc.

Credit lines for borrowed material continue on p. viii.

Library of Congress Cataloging-in-Publication Data
Dethier, Brock.
　　From Dylan to Donne : bridging English and music / Brock Dethier.
　　　　p. cm.
　　Includes bibliographical references and index.
　　ISBN 0-86709-532-6 (acid-free paper)
　　1. English philology—Study and teaching.　2. Music and literature.
3. Music in education.　I. Title.

PE66 .D48 2003
420'.71—dc21　　　　　　　　　　　　　　　　　　2002152563

Consulting editor: Lisa Luedeke
Editor: Tom Newkirk
Production: Vicki Kasabian
Cover design: Joni Doherty
Typesetter: Tom Allen, Pear Graphic Design
Manufacturing: Steve Bernier

Printed in the United States of America on acid-free paper
07 06 05 04 03 DA 1 2 3 4 5

To my mother, Maisie,
whose songs have been a soundtrack of my life;

to my father, Charles,
in whose teaching footsteps I'm proud to walk;

to Don Murray
for lighting the way.

Contents

Acknowledgments

My students, colleagues, relatives, and friends have been introducing me to new music and supplying me with inspiration, feedback, and insights for decades. I'm sure I've forgotten some of the people who have played such important roles for me, but not John Baird, Doug Baldwin, David Barlow, Andrea Barnes, Haig Brown, Steve Buzzell, Paul Cadigan, Charles Cuthbertson, my siblings David and Megan Dethier and Deborah Rockenbaugh, Mark Edson, Lester Fisher, Alice Fogel, my cousins Andrew, Jan, and Nicky Hardenbergh, John Hickenlooper, Jason Homer, Matt Irwin, Hilse Jacobsen, David Jenson, Tom Lacey, Jack Lannamann, Richard Louth, Stefan Low, Merrilyne Lundahl, Lisa MacFarlane, Sheila McNamee, Lynne McNeill, Christine Millard, Eric Nankervis, Charlie Provenzano, Peter Sable, John Sandman, Sarah Sherman, Kim Smith, Paul Stout, Jerry van Ieperen, David Watt, Jim Waychus, and Dave and Ray of No Such Animal.

Special thanks to Doug Smeath and Kate Snyder for giving me permission to print their essays, and to all my ex-students who sent me memories of the music in their classes, including Iren Bencze, Aaron Croft, Cathy Larsen, Olivia Lester, Sherilynn Moody-Bouwhuis, Jennifer Ward, and Michael Ward.

Ben F. Nelms, the editor of *English Journal* in 1991, published the article that led to this book. Bill Varner was the godfather of the book, encouraging me as we struggled to find the right slant, and Tom Newkirk kindly took over at Heinemann when Bill left. The FHE writing group helped me rethink early drafts, and my wife, Melody Graulich, was as always my best editor.

In light of the greediness of some music publishers and the refusal of others even to respond to my requests, I especially want to thank the following songwriters and music publishers for their friendliness and generosity: Tori Amos and Sword and Stone Publishing, Greg Brown and Hacklebarney Music, Jon Clark and Ringing Ear Records, Elvis Costello and Plangent Visions Music, Delta Haze Corporation, Ani DiFranco and Righteous Babe Music, Bob Dylan Music Co., Robert Hunter and Ice Nine Publishing, Janis Ian and Taosongs Two, Jefferson Airplane and Advance Party Music, Tom Lehrer, Ian MacKaye and Dischord Records, Van Morrison and Bernice Music, East Bay Ray and Decay Music, Peggy Seeger and StormKing Music, Bill Thompson.

Continued from p. ii

Introduction

*So many literary themes and techniques that might other-
wise become mired in boredom, familiarity, indifference,
irrelevance, or other obstacles to the appreciation and understanding we as English teachers hope to transfer to students
can be conveyed easily through music.*
Juanita E. Tipton, high school teacher, 1991

*Music makes for a very honest experience and it allows stu-
dents to have opinions and ideas and to feel emotions and—
what it seems most students try to avoid at all costs—it
makes us think.*
Olivia Lester, undergrad, reflecting on my use
of music in our Intermediate Writing class

Two very different stories compete for dominance in the modern
English classroom. In one, which has roots in romantic tradition,
modernism, and so-called expressivism, the writer's primary responsibility is, as sportswriter Red Smith put it, to sit in front of the keyboard
and "open a vein." Writers are loners, plumbing their experiences,
their senses, their imaginations, creating unique expressions of the
human condition, needing mostly freedom and space to do their precious work.

While the first story emphasizes individuality, volition, and
choice, the second calls them illusions. Its advocates delight in pointing out how channeled, limited, and self-censored are the ideas of the
wannabe radical individualists: not the individuals themselves but the
communities in which they have lived and worked determine their
values, their dreams, their genres, the very words they choose. These
constructionists insist that we should replace the self-indulgences of
expressivism, the illusion of autonomous selfhood, with an analysis of
the forces that have shaped students as people and writers and of the
community in and for which writers write.

Music can bridge this gap, link the two theories, the two stories,
the two versions of the writer that they create. Music can help English
teachers pursue both the pleasures of self-expression that motivate

many student writers and the constructionist goals of many current theorists. Music can provide the most effective way to introduce and explain everything from the importance of leads to the concept of unreliable narrator, from the creativity of revision to romantic irony. Each chapter of this book presents a different way in which music can help us see, understand, appreciate, and analyze aspects of writing, literature, and our world.

Why Music?

Many different subjects could help create such a bridge between individual and group, academic and real world, expression and analysis—certainly any of the arts, and almost anything that comes under the heading "popular culture," including movies and television. John Gaughan and Bruce Pirie are among the many teacher/researchers who detail how a focus on films, ads, drama, or consumer culture can advance both expressivist and constructionist agendas. Gaughan says, "I want [students] to challenge some of their assumptions and consider how those assumptions were constructed in the first place. Teaching them to read cultural texts is a start" (113).

While a knowledgeable and enthusiastic teacher could use virtually any subject productively in an English classroom, for a number of reasons music provides the ideal bridge.

■ Young people already discuss and analyze music enthusiastically. It provides a subject with which teachers, as Sheila McNamee puts it, can "engage participants in very practical activities where they bring the conversations of the classroom into a domain of their lives (either one with which they are engaged or one about which they care passionately)." Christenson and Roberts attest to the importance of music in young people's lives: "For every adult who is convinced pop music is responsible for the moral decay of our youth, there is an adolescent who believes music is the only positive force in contemporary society" (6). When asked which medium they would take to a desert island, seventh, ninth, and eleventh graders chose music over television, books, computers, video games, radios, newspapers, and magazines (33).

■ Music functions as a universal language with its own dialects, some of which students can call "mine." David Riesman writes, "by learning to talk about music, one also learned to talk about other things" (12). And says Gaughan: "If we want to break down walls between living and learning in our students' lives, we need to immerse them in topics that concern them both in and out of school" (163).

■ We can use music efficiently, without devoting a lot of class time to it. I typically start playing the song of the day two or three minutes before the class officially starts, rewarding early birds and giving everyone another reason to get to class on time. The song ends as the parade of stragglers is slowing down, I spend two or three minutes explaining how the music illuminates some class topic, and we're off. When I don't play music at the beginning of class, I'm very conscious of the dead air and dead time as the early students and I wait for late-comers. Obviously music can create a welcome break at any point in a class period, but I'm fond of opening the class with music because it wakes us all up, sets a tone and direction for the class period, and makes productive a few minutes that would otherwise be wasted. As one of my freshman students put it, "your music helped bring us into class . . . it made us sit and think, 'Now why would he choose this song—what relevance could this possibly have?' and thus gave us a great interest in the day's topic" (J. Ward).

■ What Cheryl Reed says about popular culture in general can be true of music in particular: its "main function, its inherent value to us as knowledge-makers, as writers of the coherent narratives that we call theory, is its potential to rattle us" (99). In this book, I describe how making sense of the music in my life has exposed my preconceptions and helped me to challenge my assumptions about a number of issues. While I can't guarantee that music will similarly rattle my students, I certainly cultivate that possibility.

■ Music shapes students' identity growth. It provides language and metaphors with which students make sense of their experience and leads to insights that inspire outstanding writing.

■ Music motivates. Students demand it to get psyched for the big game or to start the weekend with the proper energy. And it can change students' lives.

■ Songs can help students create and understand their personalities and personae. They provide titles, quotations, and central metaphors for introspection, discussions, and presentations.

■ Music is neutral territory; it offers an unusually open market for the fabrication and exchange of opinions, without the dominance of one opinion source. Unlike literature or art, it isn't the accepted domain of the teacher, and unlike fads, drugs, and sex practices, it isn't the private preserve of students. Teachers and students can share it. I might know more blues and jazz, but they know more pop and rap. And we can all find comfortable spaces in the huge baggy category "rock." Gaughan insists that "students' presence in school must constantly be affirmed" (17); meeting them half way with music, validating their taste, is an excellent way to provide such affirmation.

■ Students understand that taste, evaluation, and judgment about music involve both underlying principles and subjectivity. Therefore they can accept divergence of opinion without feeling threatened or dominated. My lack of interest in Britney Spears does not challenge students' passion for her. And my fondness for John Coltrane's sax playing doesn't send most of them to the CD store demanding *A Love Supreme*. Discussing matters of taste and judgment about music can lead students to a new sense of both the relativism of taste and the existence of articulable standards in other areas—notably literature.

■ Music is pleasure. I've met a few students who say they're indifferent to music, but none who associate it with suffering, as an unfortunate number of students do with English. Students perceive my playing music as an attempt to increase their pleasure. Some teachers might worry that playing music in class panders to students, but many students feel that school ignores their interests, and they can use a little educational pandering. The pleasure of music invigorates discussions and casts a glow of acceptance over even the analytical and intellectual work that we do with music. Making a point with music resembles writing by brainstorming ideas randomly on a yellow pad: it's the lowest-cost way to get something done. And the irony is I play music for my own pleasure as much as for my students'.

■ Music provides interesting analogies to all the processes of reading and writing. It involves inspiration and discipline; writing, reading, and performing; language and style and voice; sophisticated, precise notation and widely varied interpretation. Any lesson about music applies, it seems, to other forms of writing.

■ We're all musicians, just as we're all writers and readers. We might not think of ourselves in those terms, but we still sing along to oldies radio and spend three hours on that Christmas letter to friends. Everyone has skills, tastes, prejudices, beliefs about English and music.

■ Listening may be the most important and most neglected communication skill; most of us do it more than we read, write, or talk, yet we seldom receive even the most cursory training in it. ("On average, American adolescents spend somewhere between four and five hours a day listening to music and watching music videos—at least as much time as they spend watching standard television fare and more than they spend with their friends outside of school" [Christenson and Roberts, 8].) Just giving students a listening mini-exercise in every class can shape up listening "muscles" that might otherwise atrophy. Some students know very few lyrics, even to favorite songs; they tend to listen as passively to songs as they do to lecturers and other authorities. That's a tendency worth challenging and perhaps reversing.

■ Music and its elements are almost infinitely varied. Listening to music can involve emotion and intellect; the lyrical, the nonsensical, the wordless; researched knowledge and spontaneous response, happiness and sadness, simplicity and complexity.

■ Music is political. "The corporate-controlled media are now a primary, if not the primary, pedagogical force in this country, one that children encounter long before entering the public school system and one that continues to exercise its influence throughout their lives" (Ogdon, 507). Any course that deals with how and what we learn should engage with, challenge, question this "force," and music is a particularly convenient aspect of corporate-controlled media to interrogate.

As Geoffrey Sirc points out in "Never Mind the Tagmemics, Where's the Sex Pistols?," back before "compositionists" existed, a number of people who taught writing—even some who couldn't stand popular music—saw the value of music in the writing class and began exploring its various uses. Stephen Carter wrote in *CCC* back in 1969 that "the problem of getting the freshman to write something he cares about, of helping him to begin with his own springs of judgment or opinion, continues to be the biggest obstacle in a first-year English program," and he went on to argue that "there is in contemporary music a vast and rewarding writing potential for students" (228). That potential has been largely unrealized, as the discipline has focused on best methods and on training in "academic discourse." But I hope this book fills the needs and fulfills the promise that people like Carter saw thirty years ago.

Theoretical Positioning

Disciplines from English to forestry, management to anthropology are grappling with the practical classroom implications of some of the central tenets of postmodern thought: there is no single stable meaning in any text or utterance; text, writer, and reader all contribute to the creation of meaning. Meaning is, therefore, affected by a wide range of cultural and personal factors and associations; meaning is not something that teachers can preach and students can memorize.

Current pedagogical thought derides what Paulo Freire calls the *banking concept*, the idea that teachers fill empty students with knowledge, yet the dethroning of that concept leaves educators with the task of redesigning courses and pedagogy to take advantage of our present understanding of the multiplicity of meaning. What should our new classroom relationships look like, and how do we create them?

Social constructionists argue that English teachers must join the postmodern world by helping their students see that what they view as their own opinions, ideas, and frames of reference are in fact constructions of their class, race, locale, religion, and gender. Many observers predict that incorporating constructionist insights into English will not be enough and that English as a subject will evolve into cultural studies.

Though they strive to erase the boundaries between academia and The World, cultural studies and constructionism, as movements and disciplines, are intellectual esoterica on the far fringes of general knowledge. What relevance do they have to ordinary people, ordinary teachers who feel pressured by constant testing to revive the banking concept? How can we share their insights with our students?

Conversation—the oldest teaching tool of all—is the current pedagogical method of choice for creating and revealing connection and relevance, and music is the perfect conversation starter in the postmodern classroom. It is the bridge between expressivism and constructionism; it helps make the classroom into what Mary Louise Pratt calls a "contact zone . . . where cultures meet, clash, and grapple with each other" (76); it expands the boundaries of English and eases the move into cultural studies; it allows us to see "both/and" instead of "either/or." It can even help initiate students into the world of academic discourse. It may not be indispensable to current English teachers, but it's the cheapest, easiest, most fun tool we can use in our classrooms.

I am not so swept away by my subject as to suggest that the twenty-first-century English classroom should be built around music. But I do think music is uniquely suited to influence the future of English, and in twenty years we may look back and marvel at its current absence as we now marvel at the absence of women authors in the English classes of our youth.

For baby boomers, music was the contact zone and the raw material for the construction of self. (I can speak only for my generation, but perhaps this has been true since recorded music became a major source of entertainment.) When I was growing up, listening to "counterculture" music on "underground" radio, the family stereo was the battlefield where the Beatles rolled over Beethoven, and then Hendrix left them both in a purple haze. We defined ourselves by allegiances to particular genres—folk, cool jazz, heavy metal—and particular performers—the Beatles or the Stones, the Grateful Dead or the Supremes. We thought and spoke in song lyrics, and when we began to understand Vietnam, we turned to Earth Opera and Bob Dylan to express our outrage. For those of us in sheltered white communities, music provided a rare window into African American life and a way to gauge our own racism, roles it has been playing for at least a century.

Now that even "alternative" music is mainstream, the barriers that used to divide generations and genres and races are disappearing: Britney Spears is on stage with, maybe even talking to, Tony Bennett and A Tribe Called Quest and Kenny G and Abdulla Ibrahim and the New York Philharmonic and an Indian tabla master and the chord singers of the Himalayas. As Andrew Goodwin puts it, "'older' music has become contemporary for audiences of *all* ages" (259). Hit albums like Santana's 1999 *Supernatural* bring together Hispanic and Anglo, old and young; musicians collaborate, genres meld. It's hard to imagine a vehicle better suited for easing English classrooms into the postmodern world than music. Students rightly view music as one of the most expressive human endeavors, yet we can use it to advance many constructionist goals:

- putting individual expression into larger contexts
- showing how social forces, not just the artist and the audience, determine both the creation of and the reaction to a particular piece
- making students aware of the constructedness of artifacts
- leveling the hierarchies of taste and knowledge, allowing anyone to be expert and any taste to be valid
- helping students understand and gain some control over their reading and reacting processes
- seeing from the point of view of marginalized characters
- inviting resistance and divergent thinking
- giving voice to doubts
- helping students grasp the concept of an intellectual or artistic conversation: after thinking about how Arrested Development is related to Sly Stone, they may be more ready to understand the conversations between Booker T. Washington and W. E. B. DuBois or between Shakespeare and Tom Stoppard
- demonstrating how we make sense of the world through metaphor—how many millions of people think wistfully of dreams coming true "Over the Rainbow"?

Music can illuminate the constructionist perspective in so many ways partly because it so often mirrors or helps to create the culture from which it grows. It can meaningfully link individual, personal expressions with larger social and political issues.

Although I draw frequently on the insights of people like Goodwin, McNamee, and Pratt, I do not attempt to align my ideas with those of any one theorist or approach. I'm promoting a methodology through a metaphor, the bridge. I will be happy if English teachers use my methods to further aims I've never dreamed of. And I trust that everyone using this book will challenge, deconstruct, refine, amplify, extend, and perfect my ideas. This book is a part of a conversation, not a definitive manifesto.

While I hope that my ideas make sense in light of current theory, I also am dedicated to demonstrating that music serves the needs of teachers laboring under the weight of relentless testing, teachers who feel forced to emphasize content rather than process and identification rather than creation. Music enlivens, motivates, intrigues, stimulates. A student who remembers that "tone" is a key difference between Tori Amos' and Nirvana's versions of "Smells Like Teen Spirit" may have a shot at identifying the term on a multiple-choice test. The student who does the first serious research of his life to learn about the history of blues guitar playing may remember how to use the Internet and the library on the next project. The student encouraged by the playing of "Another Brick in the Wall" to discuss class problems may come out of the corner and study for the competency exam.

Music provides another classroom language, a bridge between individuals, genres, time periods, and groups. Every time I use music in class, we pay attention to some particular line, aspect, or stance— an individual expression. In the few minutes that we usually spend talking about the music of the day, we make connections between that expression and a larger context in which it is meaningful. This book explores scores of ways that the bridge of music can aid English teachers, not just to do better the work they may have been doing for years, but also to ease them into new concepts, new activities, new ways of seeing their field.

Who I Am and What I'm Not

Disclaimers first: I am not a professional musician, a musicologist, a discographer, a sociologist, a psychologist, a music educator, a theorist of culture or of literature, or a rock critic. Doing my homework for this book, I have read the work of people who write under all of those labels, and it impressed upon me the need for humility.

I *am* a composition teacher with a doctorate in English pedagogy and twenty-five years of learning from my students and from colleagues like Donald Murray. I am a white, middle-class, suburban baby boomer. I am an amateur musician: I have been singing all my life, like many of my generation I learned to play guitar when the Beatles invaded, and I have even sold a few copies of two song-and-story kids' tapes I wrote and recorded. I am, of course, a music lover, and rather than give up on the noisy rock of my youth, I find that my tastes continuously expand, adding ever more sounds that give me pleasure. I am a writer with a couple of other books to my credit, currently most fascinated with poetry. I am a political person interested in opening students' minds and in, as we modestly put it in the sixties, changing the world. And I have been experimenting with ways to use music in English classes for fifteen or twenty years.

My authority for writing this book, therefore, rests more on the confluence of my interests than on any one area of expertise. The strength of the book resides in the connections I draw between the needs of English classes, music, and various pedagogical and theoretical concepts. I agree with cultural studies practitioners who assert that *"an interrogation of self* as well as of the world of meaning and sense" (Finn, 139) is a necessary part of an undertaking like this, so much of my analysis and criticism targets myself and my culturally constructed tastes and prejudices.

Who's My Audience?

This is a book for English teachers, not for musicians. Although I hope preservice teachers can pick up some ideas from it, the ideal reader has taught for at least a year and therefore has some knowledge of the kinds of challenges that I face with music. I try not to assume any particular knowledge of music, and I think I have successfully avoided using specific musical terminology. But I also don't want to bore readers by providing a critical bio of every musician I mention. So if a reference is too skimpy to help you make use of a particular suggestion, ask your kids or your students for help, or e-mail me at Bdethier@ english.usu.edu.

While I'm not assuming readers have any particular expertise, I am writing for an imaginative audience, people who can take new ideas and transform them for their own classrooms. The time-honored process of pedagogical borrowing requires such transformation; if I use a fellow teacher's demonstration as a script, I'm going to come across as an actor, not a teacher. We need to believe in what we do and be comfortable with it. So while I suggest many activities that could be copied directly, I hope readers will in fact appropriate and make their own any of my ideas that appeal to them.

This Book Does Not

- engage in a close reading of song lyrics in an attempt to prove that lyrics should be considered poetry, though such attempts intrigue me.

- try to provide readers with an up-to-the-minute list of popular songs sure to impress ninth graders, though I wouldn't mind having such a list myself.

- advocate assigning students to write music or even write about music, though I'm glad to have students do either.

- suggest using music as background or white noise to soothe savage students, though teachers who need music for that purpose have my sincere sympathy and teachers who do it creatively have much to teach me.

- discuss music videos or dwell on my opinion that they're one of the worst things ever to happen to popular music.

- argue that rock—or any other kind of music—is inherently liberating or revolutionary or political. Rather than imagine that the mere presence of music in the classroom will improve teaching or change students' attitudes, I hope instead that music can help us teach our students to think and write a little better. Rock won't save the world, but clear thinking might.

- discuss the Mozart effect—the spate of recent claims about the value of music for developing the mental abilities of children and even fetuses. It's a fascinating subject but not central to my pedagogical goals. Readers interested in the subject might want to start with the September 2000 edition of *Music Education Journal*, which is devoted to "music and the brain."

- lean heavily on the theory of multiple intelligences. Our profession and our nation owe Howard Gardner a huge debt for making the commonsense point that intelligence is not a single, unitary attribute. Gardner's theory leads to the conclusion that some students will learn a concept better if it is presented musically rather than in more traditional ways; variety in methods of presentation corresponds to variety in methods of grasping and processing ideas. But while a musical link to material is particularly helpful, perhaps almost necessary, for certain students, it is pedagogically, psychologically, and emotionally useful for almost all students. Although music can help teachers to reach students who otherwise would be bored and disconnected in class, I do not advocate its use primarily to reach such students. Music has long been recognized as a universal language; what other justification do we need to employ it in our courses?

- describe a class built around punk or gangsta rap or indeed any kind of music. As Geoffrey Sirc writes in a recent exchange in *CCC* about punk pedagogy, "I hate to make anyone share my enthusiasms: I'd get creeped out, feeling like Allan Bloom playing students his Mozart records" (104). I play music in almost every class, but only on rare occasions does the music or the discussion it provokes take more than a few minutes of class time. My goal is to make music an effective element of my pedagogy even for students who have no interest in it. I do not pressure students to write about music; as soon as music becomes a requirement, it loses many of the benefits I've enumerated.

- attempt, as Frith and Goodwin put it, to "rescue young people's music from the contempt of the academy" (2), a task that popular culturists have been struggling with for at least fifty years. My rejection of and impatience with that contempt should be everywhere obvious, and several of my stories involve recognizing, confronting, and attacking my own musical biases, the type of blindness and assumptions upon which such academic contempt rests. But I don't see any point in arguing directly with the Allan Blooms of the world.

- aim primarily to make "academic discourse" palatable to students. One of the ways I use the bridge metaphor is to talk about how music can help ease students into academic modes of thought. I agree with those who argue that understanding the discourse of academia and learning to manipulate it for their own ends can empower students. But I resist—as do Sirc and, I imagine, thousands of other composition teachers, now often dismissed as "expressivists"—the notion that our main job is to usher students into the world of academic communication.

This Book Does

- focus on the pedagogical value of music, demonstrating how (and explaining why) music can help students understand reader response theory, think about the relationship between spontaneity and art, find fresh ideas for papers, get inspired about research, think about their own prejudices, study the uses of metaphor, see what "theme" means in Beethoven's hands, or discover that even a tired old idea can become beautiful when a genius like Coltrane works on it.

- demonstrate many different kinds of connections between English and music and suggest specific songs with which to develop those connections. Readers who aren't inspired to use some of the music they know will have no problem borrowing ideas from me. There are enough specific suggestions here to keep a teacher going for years, but those suggestions are limited by my own background, tastes, imagination, and experience: I suggest very few musical experiments that I haven't used myself. I hope to prod teachers into using their own imaginations to make their own connections with music that excites them.

- integrate politics into the discussion whenever possible. I agree with those who understand that "pedagogy cannot be divorced from politics, lived experience, or an intense sense of caring about something that really matters" (Ogdon, 501) and with George Harrison, who said, "If you've got a platform you should speak" (quoted in "Music and Politics," 61). My students are steeped in certain aspects of popular culture but most have been well trained by the dominant culture to view politics as someone else's business, best handled by those dedicated to it. They know the culture but not the politics, and I think if we're going to give them the candy of music it ought to be served with the gristle of politics.

- provoke teachers to think about what McNamee calls "the multiple ways in which teaching can take place."

- expand students' tastes and broaden their knowledge of musical eras, genres, and approaches. I'm enthusiastic about almost every song I bring to class, and while I try to play enough current music to convince students I'm still listening, I consciously draw from the far corners of my own musical taste, to provide students with as much range and diversity as possible, in hopes that a Backstreet Boys fan might listen to the Grateful Dead, and a Deadhead might listen to Billie Holiday.

- provide readers with as many resources as possible with which they can start using and enjoying music more in their classes. Besides describing actual activities, I give basic source information for every piece of music I mention, and I connect my activities to cultural, theoretical, and empirical work from many disciplines.

Teacher Worries About Using Music in Class

1. *I don't know enough about music.* We don't need to be musicians or music critics. We need just one insight, one connection between music and something happening in the class. And often that connection can be framed as a question: Why is Jimi Hendrix doing that with the

"Star Spangled Banner"? or Why did Alice Walker call her essay about horses and slavery "Am I Blue"? Our ignorance about music is in many ways an advantage, because it allows students to be the experts and teach us.

Teachers worried that their lack of musical expertise would invalidate their use of music in the classroom should read "Words and Music in the English Classroom," in which nineteen high school and college teachers discuss their own uses of music. They sing and dance and use music in ways I have never dreamed of. Creativity is the prerequisite, not musical knowledge. As Beth Cox of Chichester High School puts it, "the worse I sing the more I captivate my audience" (77).

2. *I'm 30 years out of date; the last album I bought was* Crosby, Stills & Nash. Your students will enjoy introducing you to more recent music, and some of them may be knowledgeable and astute enough to supply you with appropriate songs if you ask, for instance, for an example of radical revision in music or of lyrics that might be considered poetry. I explain throughout this book the value of analyzing and facing the ways in which our musical choices mirror who we are.

We have to keep in mind the difference between musical knowledge and literary knowledge. As English teachers, we're expected to know more than most people about books and sentences, so many of us develop paranoia about being found out—that we've never read *Moby Dick* or don't know what a gerund is. But knowing the origins of hip hop is not part of our job description, and students assume we're ignorant about music unless we're very young and very hip. Students need to hear authorities say "I don't know" in class. Saying it about music is safe.

Teachers who prefer Chopin or Calloway to Cobain can take heart from a study, "Music Style Preferences of Different Age Listeners" (LeBlanc, Sims, Sivola, and Obert), that probed listeners' reactions to jazz, rock, and "art music" (what most of us would call classical). While jazz was consistently (though narrowly) the least preferred of the three genres, art music outscored rock for a number of different age groups, including (to my surprise) ninth through eleventh graders. While both jazz and classical music have been marginalized in the musical marketplace, evidently they have not lost their inherent appeal. Most of my examples come from the huge, baggy category that is rock, but I strongly encourage teachers to draw their own examples from their own musical enthusiasms. Students' interest in non-cutting-edge music may be latent, but apparently it exists. (The study also, incidentally, confirmed the widely held impression that sixth through eighth graders are the hardest-to-please age group.)

3. *The music they're making these days isn't worth listening to.* If you feel this way, you're in for a treat if you start discussing music with your students and opening your ears to their favorites. Sure, frothy imitation rules, but people you've never heard of are recording a tremendous amount of good music. You just have to find it.

4. *I don't know what my students are listening to.* They'd probably love to tell you. When I was growing up, it was possible at least to imagine that one person could know all the new music coming out. Now it clearly isn't. As Michael Jarrett writes, "While reissues make us omniscient in theory, enabling us to hear anything and everything we want to hear, they make us ignorant in practice. Never before have we felt so finite or heard less of what's available" (43). So join the crowd.

5. *I don't know how to analyze music.* Any teacher who wishes to do so can, with a few minutes of thought and perhaps a few more of listening to appropriate music, become more adept at musical analysis than most students. Throughout this book, I discuss ways in which musical analysis resembles literary analysis. Most of the time, I talk about how analyzing a song can teach us something about reading or writing, but teachers worried about analyzing music need to realize that the process is reversible: the techniques of analyzing texts can be fruitfully applied to analyzing music.

All English teachers are experts in using such techniques—we know how to define, categorize, compare, move between whole and parts, look at cause and effect, explore contexts, develop meanings, and ask intelligent questions. So even a teacher with very little musical background in a class of avid rap fans should not feel intimidated and can still use many of the suggestions in this book. The key is to be honest, not try to fake interest or expertise where none exists, but also not shrink from asking of music the same kinds of questions we'd ask of a poem or a short story. Even the most basic observations about a piece of music can lead class discussion onto a potentially productive path: Why, for instance, do you focus on the lyrics in a particular song when students hear mostly bass and drums?

6. *I can't convince myself that popular culture is a legitimate subject of academic study.* Though I focus critical, scholarly attention on popular music in virtually every class I teach, I can't completely convince myself either; we're so subtly trained to see a gulf between high art

and popular art that I have vague forebodings of E. D. Hirsch Jr., who was on my doctoral orals committee, revoking my degree when he hears that I spent class time talking about punk rockers who didn't make it into his *Dictionary of Cultural Literacy*. I think we all need, in Stephen Tatum's words, to "cease demonizing the popular and begin considering how at times in even the most seemingly retrograde popular texts critical thinking about ideals, drives, contradictions, and prospects can and does occur" (164).

7. *Kids don't pay attention to lyrics*. They can use all the practice they can get. As Barrett and colleagues put it,

> Another compelling reason for including music in classrooms relates to its potential for cultivating perception. . . . In a world bombarded with sound, students must learn to listen with focused attention and intelligence. (18)

I like to emphasize the nonlyrical parts of music when I can, but I also like to prod students to listen better and pay closer attention. And if I want them to pick up on more than just a phrase, I'll put some of the words on an overhead or hand them out.

This may be as good a place as any to discuss the thorny issue of song copyrights. I would love to quote the relevant lines every time I mention a song. But for reasons I don't fully fathom, you can't quote from a Bob Dylan song as easily as you can quote from a Dylan Thomas poem. Even though this is an academic book from a small educational press unlikely to sell enough copies to buy me a new set of speakers, some copyright holders want big bucks—the Rolling Stones' minimum is $1,500—to let me quote even small snippets of song lyrics. Others refuse permission or simply don't respond. So I paraphrase much more than I would like to. Almost all song lyrics are available on the Internet, and I have included the URLs of websites for a few crucial lyrics. Copyright holders often put material on the Web to make it accessible to others, but they don't give up their reproduction rights by putting material in this medium. Sometimes copyright owners include copying guidelines on their site. Look for those as they may sometimes grant permission for noncommercial uses.

There is also a difference between official artist/publisher websites and those put up by some fans. The person who posted the material may not own any rights (as in the case of some fans' sites).

If teachers want to hand out copies of lyrics to students, they should refer to the Guidelines for Educational Uses of Music (www.musiclibraryassoc.org/copyright/). These guidelines were written by representatives of the music industry as well as educators to help clarify fair use as it applies to classroom use. They state that "for academic purposes other than performance, single or multiple copies of excerpts of works may be made . . . but in no case more than 10 per-cent of the whole work. The number of copies shall not exceed one copy per pupil." Other fair use education guidelines mention that the copying should also not be repeated with respect to the same item by the same teacher from term to term. Teachers should refer to these Educational Fair Use Guidelines for further information.

8. I don't want to give up control of class time to let students play DJ. I won't ask you to. I've found that only exceptional students can make a com-prehensible point with music in the few minutes that I want to allot to a musical connection each day. I've been privileged to learn from the musical tastes and insights of twenty-five years of students; they've been a major force in the development of my current musical knowledge. And I would gladly teach a course in which music was an accepted part of the content, so students could regularly rap and write. But in most of my classes—and, I assume, in most American English classes at every level—music is, of necessity, a means not an end, a bridge not a grail.

Getting the Music into Your Classroom

The technical and legal aspects of musical reproduction are changing so rapidly that I hesitate to go into much detail about how actually to bring music into the classroom. But here are a few thoughts for those who have never tackled this task.

I keep my own combination cassette-and-CD boom box in my office. The latest one cost fifty dollars, part of which I wrote off on my taxes as a business expense. I would hate having to count on my col-leagues to return the department's one boom box on time and in working order. For teachers experimenting with bringing music to class, borrowing a box makes sense, but once you get hooked, you'll want your own.

We make the best connections with, and think of the best exam-ples from, our own music collections, no matter how small, outdated, or idiosyncratic. So I would advise spending your time thinking of ways to use the music you have available, rather than hunting down some possibly obscure track that I mention. But if you want to use the music suggested in this book or in other sources, you have a wide variety of options.

- First, ask students. If no one owns the desired song on disk or tape, chances are someone loves to download music off the Internet (from one of the legal sites).

- Try the library. You might be surprised at what it carries.
- Try downloading. Your students can probably point you to the current best sites; a search for "download music" will turn up plenty. This might be a good time to discuss Napster and the issues of "free" music on the Internet.
- If you're willing to pay for a CD, you can almost certainly find the song you want. The bibliography lists a source for every song I mention in the book, sometimes with two dates—the original release date and the date of the anthology or re-release. But record companies like Rhino comb the music of the past so thoroughly to make anthologies and revivals that you may find a readily available source for your song different from the one I mention. On sites such as www.amazon.com, www.cdnow.com/, www.rhino.com/, and Collector's Choice (www.ccmusic.com), you can search by writer, performer, song title, and sometimes words from the song. And your local used CD store or www.half.com may well have the disk you're looking for at half the retail cost.
- To find who performed a particular version of a song, try the websites maintained by the companies that keep track of copyrights and royalties for musical artists: ASCAP (http://ascap.com/) and BMI (http://bmi.com/home.asp). The All Music website, www.allmusic.com/, also has an impressive search engine.
- Lyrics are usually very easy to find. Type "[artist's name] song lyrics" into your search engine, and you're almost certain to find good links.
- Boom boxes aren't nearly as prone to disastrous shutdowns as laptops and other classroom audiovisual aids, but spending time fast-forwarding through a tape, trying to find a particular song, will put any class to sleep. So I always cue the tape before class, and if I want to play two or three things from tape during one class, I'll retape them one after the other, so I don't have to spend time searching.

A Note About Chapter Format

Each chapter opens with quotations, often from theorists, because I want to keep reminding readers that the often-playful use I make of music *is* theoretically grounded. Teachers whose use of music is challenged by parents or administrators will, I hope, turn to these quotations and to the sources noted throughout the text for theoretical and pedagogical justification and support. I have often included the original date of publication of the quotations, rather than the date of the collection they appear in, to provide as much historical context as possible.

Following the epigraphs, I have included, in italics, a brief overview and introduction to the chapter. Each chapter has its own perspective and focus, but the chapters are not intended to be coherent, linear arguments. Sometimes the individual sections within a chapter are tied together thematically, while in other chapters, the sections present a dozen different and largely unrelated examples of the chapter's general emphasis. Always, readers should keep in mind the reminders that follow this introduction.

Every chapter closes with a specific suggestion for a writing assignment. Many of the activities I discuss throughout the book involve writing, but I have used the chapter-ending assignments to ensure that I have connected and made concrete the chapter's concerns. The assignments are not meant to be summative, tying together all of the chapter's ideas, but suggestive, inspiring teachers to create their own assignments to fulfill the purposes of the chapter. In most cases the assignments build on the musical prompts suggested throughout the chapter, but usually the assignment itself does not require musical prompts or analysis.

Please Read This

Every time you start reading a new chapter or finish a particular example, please remind yourself of the following points, which apply virtually everywhere in this book. If I can count on you to remember these points, I won't bore you by repeating them every page.

1. My examples come from my admittedly limited background; therefore
2. You should substitute your own examples whenever possible.
3. Even better, ask your students and peers to suggest examples (but see more on this in the Introduction).
4. My main purpose is to demonstrate a wide variety of ways that music can be used in English classes. I hope to inspire other teachers both to imitate and to innovate. So getting you to agree on a particular element of content—to accept, for instance, my stance on misreadings—is less important to me than convincing you to try using music to explain a stance of your own. What I have to offer you is a process—a way of making connections and of rethinking English pedagogy.

One

Constructing Identity

The language and images of a culture shape identity.
                    Tom Romano, English professor and
                    promoter of multigenre writing, 1997

Identity has become central to modern education. At least since the upheavals of the 1960s, English classes have been encouraging students to express themselves, explore themselves, determine who they are and want to be and to write about things that matter to them. More recently, such exploration has been extended to include examination of where our sense of self comes from, what has shaped us and made us who we are. This relatively new focus is necessary, advocates say, to give students a more complete answer to "Who am I?" and to help them appreciate the views and beliefs of people from very different backgrounds. This chapter details a number of ways music can help students explore and express their inner landscapes as well as see in larger contexts themselves and the forces that have shaped them.

Why Analyze Music?

What are you listening to? What's in your CD player at the moment? What tune is bouncing around your head? What do you hope comes on the radio on your drive home?

I ask students to jot down an answer to these questions as I turn on Neil Young's "Down by the River." It's early in the semester. This activity provides a rationale for all my musical analysis, so I play the

1

song in almost every composition and literature class and workshop. I want to demonstrate both the value of analyzing the music in our lives and the importance of music in reflecting, revealing, and sometimes creating our own identities. I want to convince students that analysis is not just for people who want to understand Shakespeare but benefits all people who want to understand themselves and their interests. I want to give students practice in academic thought.

Before I ask students to take a critical look at the course texts— which they're likely to perceive as alien, highbrow, teacher texts— I have them read critically in a genre many of them treasure: music. Before they reflect on how their upbringing influences their reading, they think about how their background led to the choice of the tunes in their head. Before they choose—in desperation or for lack of imagination—a teacher subject to write on, they test drive a subject or two embedded in their current musical fixation. I want them to use music as a bridge between their experiences and those of the English course, between their personal expression and the academic writing they'll soon be asked to do, between their own cherished sense of individuality and the many contexts that have helped shape them.

Analyzing our musical choices reveals ourselves to ourselves, giving us insight and some control over our identity-forming processes. Our choices, our tastes reflect some part of us. Sometimes when we interrogate them, what we discover can be alarming.

In 1969, "Down by the River," off Neil Young's much-anticipated second solo album, spoke directly to my lonely male adolescence. The narrator is alone, reaching out for connection. An unhappy seventeen-year-old at the time, I swooned at the thought that the "she" in the song could "drag" the narrator "over the rainbow." Like, I think, most teenage males (or most teenagers?), I felt that I was romantically hopeless (and therefore by a cruel irony hopelessly romantic), and the song held open the possibility that there might be a girl somewhere sometime who could drag me out of that state, over the rainbow, and to the pot of gold—a blissful relationship.

It took me ten years to stop swooning and realize what the song is about: homicide. This guy isn't some pacifistic poem-writing romantic; he shoots her. Dead. No metaphor there. Ooops.

Pick up any American newspaper on any given day and you'll find a story or two about husband, boyfriend, ex-husband, ex-boyfriend knocking on some woman's door and blowing her away because she wouldn't drag him over some rainbow. Well past the time when Mother fixes all the boo-boos, men in our culture run to the women in their lives to fix their broken heads. In my most romantic heart-of-hearts, I was desperately looking for a woman to fix me, thinking like a wife killer!

That realization had a profound effect on me. For one thing, it led me to back off every time I find myself engaging in "Down by the River" thinking. I have to stop myself and say, "It's not her job, it's mine. I've got to make my own rainbows." I now see such thinking all around me, and I try to expose it for what it is. Somewhere in the historical development of modern gender roles, men seem to have given over to women the role of emotional rescuer, source of comfort and contentment. Even feminist men often hold women responsible for some aspect of their happiness. That burden of responsibility no doubt crushes many relationships even if it doesn't produce violence.

In terms of its relevance to an English class, the more important lesson I learned from this experience is that making sense of your musical preferences can teach you about much more than music, can in fact change your life. If I had never analyzed my attachment to that song, I might never have confronted an important and unfair assumption that many men live by. My relationships would have suffered. And because my revelation about "Down by the River" led me to scrutinize my other tastes and attachments for similar insights, it has affected my life ever since in countless ways.

After describing all that I gained from analyzing "my" song, I ask students to write about the song that they jotted down at the beginning of class. Is there an event or relationship associated with it? Does it express some personally important idea or feeling at the moment, "I'm So Lonesome I Could Cry" (Williams) or "I am not a pretty girl / that's not what I do" (DiFranco)? Do you keep coming back to a line from the chorus, a beat you like to dance to, an image the song paints in your head? Have you ever tried to put all the pieces of the song together to see if you can speculate about what the songwriter had in mind?

For many students, this quick peek into their musical interests remains just a small entry in their class notes. And that's fine; I usually sequence course assignments to move from personal to more expository, impersonal, and academic, and if they've been intrigued by this kind of personal analysis or have gained confidence in their analytical abilities by seeing that they can analyze music, they'll be more ready to step toward more traditional academic reading, writing, and analysis. But some are interested enough to follow an initial insight with serious analysis and self-scrutiny. Many excellent papers have resulted from this three-minute initial probe into musical taste; some students are compelled to figure out why they like the song, what it's doing in their heads. And I trust that after this experience, when my students start to dismiss their interest in a song—or a painting or a movie or a person—with "Oh, I just like it," at least some stop to ask themselves, "Is it really that simple?"

For writing activities that grow from this initial prompt, see Write: Self-Analysis at the end of this chapter and Write: Beyond the Individual at the end of Chapter 2.

Students' Identity Growth Through Music

Besides providing quick and easy access to writers' inner life, music helps shape the identity growth of a large number of my students, and making music part of the conversation in English class gives students the opportunity and emotional space to acknowledge and articulate its influence. Music is *their territory*. As they ponder what it means to them and try to determine why it's so important, they develop critical reading skills that they can use on any "text."

The prompt with which I began this chapter—pick a current favorite song and try to figure out why that choice is meaningful—led Doug to write a prize-winning essay about his discovery of Tori Amos' music (see Appendix A). He showed how Amos' music and philosophy had helped him to accept himself and his own homosexuality, to believe that his difference might not be a bad thing. The spark for Doug was an Amos line about someone who had been "everybody else's girl" but never her own. Doug related to the character, as would many teens undergoing a period of alienation, and the more he thought about what being his own person meant, the more radical his split from the norm became and the more confident he felt about the person he was becoming. Writing to explore and perfect, Doug revised well past A, as he articulated his obsession with Amos and his own evolving sense of self. I can't claim that Doug changed as a result of the writing, but I know he was grateful for a chance to put into coherent form the central development of his life.

Amy was only seventeen, working as a canvasser for a nonprofit group, when her boss pressured her into sleeping with him. When she discovered that the boss had seduced other underage coworkers, she at first felt shame and confusion, and, like many girls in such a situation, blamed herself. But as she walked from house to house, she listened to a portable CD player, and the angry, biting, assertive music of PJ Harvey became her favorite. She listened to the outrage in "Sheela-Na-Gig," in which the man rebukes the woman's recital of her "charms" by calling her an "exhibitionist," and she borrowed from the song "Dry" the ultimate putdown of male sex partners. As she reconstructed that summer in her paper, Amy realized that Harvey's music had played an important role in turning shame into anger and anger into action: she eventually reported her boss to his superiors, and he was fired.

Musical prompts can also help students deal with trauma in their lives and understand who they have become as a result of it. Kristin wrote about her fondness for Simon and Garfunkel's "I Am a Rock" because it was her theme song during her parents' divorce, inspiring her to find the strength she needed. Kate Snyder began her essay "The Green Pillows" (see Appendix B) just weeks after her mother's death. She didn't intend to write about her mother; it was too soon, and the musical prompt led her first to her father, the biggest influence on her musical taste. When she was young, he would cue a record for her, help her put on the headphones, and arrange the green pillows for her comfort. Kate enjoyed the subject, in part because at first it took her into a happier time in her life and diverted her attention from her mother's recent death. But as she developed the draft, Kate realized she was less interested in writing about the music than about the green pillows, which represented stability during the time of excruciating loss and change. Reading "The Green Pillows," you'd never know it developed from a musical prompt, and yet I don't think Kate would have written the essay without the music.

Occasionally, a musical prompt opens the door to an obsession and career. I gave Dave his first chance to write about music in my Prose Writing class; he reviewed Cream's *Wheels of Fire*, and his fascination with lyrics and the minutiae of production made the piece valuable even for a reader who'd been listening to the album for fifteen years. The last I heard of Dave, he had moved to Los Angeles, had his own jazz show, and was writing music reviews.

My most overt attempt to get students to use music as an identity probe is the "stranded" assignment. In *Stranded*, a book edited by Greil Marcus, twenty rock critics answer the question, What rock and roll record would you take to a desert island? I modify the question somewhat, insisting that students choose a commercially available compact disk and providing them with plenty of canned meat and cheese spread for their island stay. Being forced to choose only *one* and to justify the choice is torture for some students. As individuals and as a whole class, we grapple with questions that would make a constructionist happy:

- Why did you choose that one album?
- What does it say about you?
- What in your background led to that choice?
- What were the runners-up, and what meanings would you attach to them?

- Is there a difference between "favorite album" and "album you could listen to every day for three years"?
- How is the choice affected by the peculiarities of the situation?

Some students pass up their favorite album because they don't want to grow sick listening to it too much. Others choose relatively obscure CDs because they feel that the albums fit with the mood of overwhelming loneliness or with the sounds of surf and breeze in the palm trees. One young woman decided not to bring any music at all, preferring to learn to appreciate nature's music. Some focus on the importance of memory and human connection in determining their choices—they take the CD that was popular when they first fell in love or that reminds them of the loved one they would most miss. Others choose an album by a group they can think of as their friends and companions, people who will understand them. A few realize that they are glad for the escape from politics and the warped priorities of modern America, and they choose a particular CD because they want to do the kind of thinking that the music provokes. Some are eminently practical: one chose a Richard Simmons workout tape, figuring she'd lose a few pounds during her stay. All students who have written that assignment have, I believe, learned something about themselves in the process, and for many, the insights are surprising, providing the first glimpses of how much their characters are determined, constructed, by their background and social milieu.

Once students have made at least a provisional "stranded" choice, the possibilities for in-class activities based on that choice are virtually infinite. Students (and teachers) can use the musical choice to experiment with almost any approach to writing about literature or other subjects. For instance, in one class period, I might give students each of the following prompts; we write about each for four or five minutes, then discuss that activity briefly before moving on to the next.

- Freewrite on why you made your choice.
- Pick a favorite song on your chosen album and brainstorm its attractions.
- List elements of the song and/or album that stand out: melody, harmony, rhythm, lyrics, musical virtuosity, energy, variety, and so on.
- Pick one (or more) of those elements and write a paragraph about it, conveying as much detail as possible.
- Write a topic or thesis sentence in which you relate some of the details about a particular element to your overall reasons for choosing the album.

- Jot down some questions or pieces of information that you'd need to research in order to do a thorough job of discussing your chosen album.
- Read your sentence to a small peer group, then record their questions and expressions of interest.

Once familiar with such a process, students can easily apply it to literature. Substitute *book* or *story* for *album* or *song,* and they're on their way.

Undergraduates fascinate us because many are so young, growing and changing so quickly. Few would without prompting talk about their identities under construction, yet opening a door to that kind of conversation with music often yields papers about such construction and music's role in it, papers that participate in the very processes that they describe.

Constructing Myself

> One thing I've learned is that we can let others "construct" us—label us, define us, tell us who we are—or we can participate in that construction ourselves. (Gaughan, 8)

Like my students, I construct my identity partly through my musical choices. Unlike them, I do it publicly. From the first seconds of the first day of class, music helps me create a class persona. Actually, students wonder what's going on as soon as I enter class with my ubiquitous boom box. I'm sure I'm known in some student circles as the guy who plays music in his classes. Obviously I don't want to be known as *just* that, but if my appearance with a boom box initially confuses students and starts them rethinking what an English class is all about, I'm content.

Choosing the music of the day is a complex process, involving considerations of scores of different ways that the music might relate to the class activities. Before I hit the play button I also ponder at least briefly what the selection says about me. I always make an intellectual connection between the day's music and something happening in class, but the music also always reflects me. Is it the fifth white male song in a row, requiring an exploration of unconscious sexism and of the ways our upbringing limits what we know? Will they expect me to show up with a safety pin through my cheek after I've played three punk songs in the last two weeks? Which of the many Vietnam songs best represents my current view? Have I played enough recent music so that students don't think I'm a hopelessly outdated fogy, but not so much that they think I'm trying too hard to be cool?

Constructing myself with music is fun and provides a certain amount of freedom, but it also shows how identity is not completely fluid and malleable. I cannot become Rappin Brock overnight; if I pretend to have hip-hop expertise, true aficionados will spot me right away, and it's better to be ignorant than fraudulent. I can try to expand, modify, stretch, and build my musical identity, but over the course of a semester, my musical choices reveal my basic demographics: middle-class suburban white male who grew up in the 1960s and went to a boys' prep school and then to California.

I share with my students my choosing process and show how much of what I consider "my taste" has been determined by my background and the contexts I put myself in. We were a revolutionary— or was that reactionary?—generation, so we generally ignored or rejected the classical and big band tastes of our parents. Because I was growing up outside Philadelphia, I was more familiar with New York's Jay and the Americans than with L.A.'s Frank Zappa and the Mothers of Invention, and I knew Philly's Mandrake Memorial before friends turned me on to San Francisco's Grateful Dead. My students can see me as evidence both of how we have been constructed and of how the consciousness of our own constructedness can help us alter the ways we are perceived and perceive ourselves. My message, time and again, is "see how this analysis reveals the forces that have shaped my tastes and perceptions? What has shaped yours?"

Many of my peers' musical tastes have been controlled and limited by the era we grew up in; they stopped listening to new music when they graduated from college. (Hence the popularity of oldies radio stations.) Students who were monitoring my musical tastes when I first started teaching wouldn't let that happen; they persuaded me to get with it, and ever since, I have made sure to listen to at least some music not more than a decade old. I have a secret weapon for creating a teaching identity with music: my own tapes. I've written and professionally recorded two kids' song-and-story tapes, from which I play a song as part of my introduction to a new class. The lighthearted friendliness of my own songs contrasts with the serious, angry music I sometimes play, and my songs reveal me as a father and as amateur-musician-having-fun, complicating my identity in students' minds, a healthy thing for students used to thinking of their teachers as nothing more than the professional roles they play.

When I play in class "Let's Go Back the Way We Came" from one of my kids' tapes, I can use it as a springboard into much more than just a revelation of identity. I write on the board the names of my musical collaborators, and I can talk about the joys of collaboration, particularly with my astonishingly talented musical friend, Steve

Buzzell. I can present the tape as an example of how I write something big: I break it up into pieces and get down the gist of an idea for each piece before I start drafting any one of them. Or I can present the song as evidence for an obvious but often overlooked truth—our best subjects are usually close at hand.

Of course most English teachers don't have tapes of themselves to offer, but they have poems or stories or pictures that either have artistic validity of their own or can be used to demonstrate analytical thinking. Any time we can add our own creations to the mix of information students piece together about us, we can add to our validity as writers. And we can demonstrate the power that writing offers for establishing and altering our public personae.

Acquiring Tastes

Our selves and our personae are not fixed, static. Both students and teachers change, grow, and expand. Music mirrors that growth, but it can also provoke it. Consciously encouraging that process can help students glimpse their potential for growth in a number of areas, something I'd like them to tap for the rest of their lives.

I turn on X's "The World's a Mess, It's in My Kiss" and watch eagerly for response. Students frown or recoil. They're usually too polite to say anything about it, but I know many of them are thinking, Why can't she sing?

I know because I felt that way for a long time myself. In the early 1980s, a student whose writing and musical taste I admired lent me a copy of X's second album, *Wild Gift*, and said, "This is the band." I taped it, and for over a year, whenever I could stand it, I'd play the tape and tell myself if I ever got to like the grating, off-key singing of Exene Cervenka, I would certainly have lost my mind. But finally, it took: something hooked me, a song got stuck in my head, and soon I was playing it because I wanted to hear it, not because I felt I ought to.

The something in this case was Billy Zoom's guitar. I blocked out the singing just to listen to his commanding power chords and peppy fills. But then I found myself singing along, and before long I was marveling at the weird harmonies of Exene and bassist John Doe as they sang about the difficulties and then the dissolution of their love affair.

In other cases the "something" that makes me want to listen could be a catchy bass-and-drums rhythm, lively backup singing or a phrase repeated with an amusing tone. I'm not talking here about songs I'd hear on the radio and decide on the spot to add to my collection. I'm concerned with the more mysterious process of acquired tastes, and what it says about us as individuals constructing our identities.

I assume that everyone over a certain age has acquired tastes, by which I mean that, usually as the result of some internal or external pressure, the individual grows to like something that at first provoked nothing but negative feelings. I've acquired tastes for blue cheese dressing, whole wheat bread, swordfish, enchiladas, Bob Marley, cross-country skiing, NPR. Sometimes my aunt was applying the pressure, saying, "Just try a bite" until I did. (She did *not* win me over to beef tongues.) Sometimes it was friends saying, "You gotta listen to this." Often though the pressure was internal, as it was when I began writing this book and thought, I have to get less ignorant about rap. So I asked anyone with interest in rap to recommend things that I should listen to. And when the second musical friend said, "listen to A Tribe Called Quest," I finally did so in a way that I could hear what I hadn't heard before. Then a friend lent me Lauryn Hill, and after listening unimpressed on the drive home, I caught "I Used to Love Him" in the driveway and sat in the parking lot until it was over, marveling at the singing and the harmonies.

Some people worry about brainwashing students with a flood of our own tastes, but I see little danger of that. Students often find my enthusiasm for Bob Dylan amusing, and they're not about to be persuaded that he sings well. I don't know of any student who converted to punk because I played some in my class. I want to be a salesman for the process, not for a particular goal. I cheer the acquiring of new tastes, even if they're tastes I don't share.

Constructing My Class

Music also plays a major role in building an identity for my course. Playing music at the beginning of every class becomes a ritual that many students appreciate and look forward to. It's the thread that ties many classes together, and both my students and I remember class discussions and events in terms of the music for the day. When trying to re-create a train of thought about multiple readings and meanings, for instance, rather than recall it as the day we read Louise Rosenblatt, we're more likely to remember "the day we talked about misreading the Green Day song."

At first, the music adds a bit of confusion, tension, perhaps even cognitive dissonance. Is this the right class? What's rock music doing in an English class? The boom box establishes immediately that this class will be different; it will require a new kind of listening. Although most students don't yet understand the broader meaning of the word *text*, by the end of the first class they know that we're going to go beyond the classics, in fact beyond the printed word, to find material to "read" (listen to, perhaps view) and study in this English class. A course and a professor who take rock music seriously might value other unorthodox things, might find almost anything worthy of analysis.

Whatever initial conclusions students draw from the music, they're likely to generalize that they're not in Kansas anymore. I do not put down other English teachers or set myself up as the cool eccentric music lover. But I do want to illuminate and alter attitudes and assumptions. I want literature students to be asking, What is worth studying?, What is literature?, What makes some literature great?, and Why don't we read sci-fi and Stephen King in English class? I want writing students to throw out their preconceptions about research papers and rethink their attitudes toward revision. I want all students to ask Why? every time they notice they're responding emotionally to something, and I want them to learn to analyze that emotional response, articulate it, maybe even make it into a thesis. I want to be seen not as one who professes truths and knows the answers but as an enthusiastic participant in the processes that students too are engaged in—reading, writing, making meaning, discovering what works.

If students see literature as removed from their lives and alien, or if they view writing as something you only do in school, I want them to reconsider. I don't call for public confessions, but I know after studying music in a number of different ways, many students start to say to themselves, I can do this analysis stuff. In fact, I do it all the time. I just didn't realize that talking about music and trying to make sense of lyrics was analysis. Music and a little cognitive dissonance can shake up all those attitudes and encourage students to start fresh in their thinking.

While all this can happen in the first day or so of class, over a semester the music I play reflects and constructs some of my most cherished values: diversity (of genre, time period, culture, approach, gender, race, voice), open-mindedness, enthusiasm, musical energy. Consciousness of the course and self I create through musical choices helps me fine-tune and update those creations. I can't afford to get too out of touch.

Analyzing the Construction of a Professional Identity

Professional musicians develop a musical identity out of the elements of their own musical influences and interests. The more radical, original, and influential the performer, the louder the assertion of identity tends to be. John Lydon claims that the inspiration for the persona he created as the Sex Pistols' lead singer, Johnny Rotten, came from Laurence Olivier's Richard III, "the most vile character [he]'d ever seen" (Flanagan 1994, 7). Studying such a construction of professional identity can help students better understand themselves, people around them, and more generally the ways we use words and images to create any effect.

I'm particularly fond of the statement made by Patti Smith—for my money the first real punk musician—in her debut album, *Horses*, released in 1975. The opening cut remakes Van Morrison's "Gloria," one of the most widely copied songs of the 1960s, the classic *male* tribute to a girlfriend who "makes me feel all right" (Them).

Smith's version starts out with slow, ominous piano, and an opening line as audacious as any I know, declaring her independence from two thousand years of Christian thought. While Smith keeps Morrison's chorus (though speeding it up as the song progresses, giving it the insistent energy of good punk), she weaves her own narrative around it. The object of affection is still female, but so, it seems, is the narrator. Perhaps the characters are, as the liner notes put it, "beyond race gender baptism." The song transforms sexual drive and passion into music as effectively as any of the male versions of "I Want You," yet it is done by a woman, a newcomer. From this audacious beginning, Smith went on to develop a musical identity so strong that it could survive a series of *Saturday Night Live* parodies by Gilda Radner.

Why is such a self-creation relevant to students who will never stand on a stage or pick up a microphone? It both encourages students to look back at where they came from, what formed their character and tastes, and gives them a sense of the malleability of human character. Undergraduates, especially those of traditional college age, often see in their first few months of college the best chance they've ever had to leave behind their high school identities, the labels of "jock" or "air head," and create a new identity, something they can be proud of. Seeing how musicians create themselves can give them courage to try such creation and can provide models that they might imitate.

Students undergoing rapid changes, feeling pressure from many sides, can also learn from and relate to musicians whose lifestyle and identity seem forced on them, out of their control. Music can painfully illuminate our inability to change despite our awareness that we need to, a dilemma that traps many young people. The release in 1993 of Janis Joplin's first recorded song, "What Good Can Drinkin' Do," showed that the nineteen-year-old Joplin already saw clearly, and felt powerless against, the destructiveness of the drink-and-drug lifestyle that would kill her eight years later.

Songs that change or adjust a musician's musical identity can provide a more positive take on the possibility of controlling identity. More than thirty years after his death, Jimi Hendrix lives on in popular culture, and most students know him for the extremes of his act or his wild, cranked-up guitar pyrotechnics. So it's fun to play the opening of Hendrix's "Little Wing"—perhaps the only heavy guitar player's song that features the triangle-like sound of orchestra bells—and see if they can reconcile its quiet beauty to the images of Hendrix the performer burning his guitar on stage. That song could start a discussion of how it's possible for both the famous and the not-so-famous to get trapped by an identity, whether it's "heavy guitar wizard" or the familiar high school "geeks," "motorheads," and "brains." The song shows that breaking out of an identity may take a boldly beautiful move.

John Lennon made such a move when he recorded the *Plastic Ono Band* album following his primal scream therapy. The album explores the identity of someone very famous yet still quite young and in some ways unsure of himself. Playing the song "God" provides a useful lead into discussions of students' own beliefs, where they come from, how they're influenced, whether they're based on religious precepts, how they might inspire writing. Lennon sheds and denies the belief systems of his time and culture, listing what he doesn't believe in, rejecting religions, politicians, musicians, Presley, Dylan, even the Beatles, but finally affirming his belief in himself. It's a good place for writing students to start.

Write: Self-Analysis

Much of the writing students do in my classes involves constructing an identity. They retell a story from their past and present themselves as more introspective and sensitive than the person their present friends know. Or they do a research paper on anorexia from the point of view of a survivor, not a victim. In a reading response paper, one takes an approach opposite to that of most of the class and establishes himself as a rebel, a nonconformist. Another, inspired by the activity at the beginning of this chapter, lends me a Radiohead CD and asserts himself as a class source of musical taste.

But the most important identity-creating writing they do, the closest they come to emulating the kind of self-defining writing they can see in songwriters, is usually the last assignment, the self-analysis. Depending on the course, they might analyze themselves as teachers, critics, or readers, but they always analyze themselves as writers. And I insist that they include their strengths. That requirement alone challenges many students. By the age of eighteen, almost everyone knows their writing weaknesses and shortcomings, but few have ever been told their strengths, and almost no student has ever before asserted in writing, "I am good at . . . ." Before they write the assignment, we brainstorm as a class some widely diverse strengths—fast typing, ability to get by on little sleep, good with metaphors, lives with excellent in-house editor.

I also ask that their self-analyses cohere in some way, so they end up writing about their evolution as a writer, or how their strengths and weaknesses are two sides of the same character trait, or how their outstanding ability as a writer and a student is organization. Confessing their strengths and trying to find some coherence to the story of their writing leads students to identify and construct "myself-as-writer." Thus they start the semester using music to analyze their identity, and they end it by taking control and asserting a writing identity.

Two

Understanding Ourselves

Like your fingerprints, your signature, and your voice, your choices of music and the ways you relate to music are plural and interconnected in a pattern that is all yours, an "idio-culture" or idiosyncratic culture in sound.
> Susan D. Crafts, Daniel Cavicchi,
> and Charles Keil, *My Music,* 1993

Constructivist teachers want students to understand that even their individuality is socially constructed: "one's sense of 'self' is made possible through the essentially social iden-tifications—family, home, country, culture, religion, gender, ethnicity—in terms of which selfhood defines itself."
> John Gaughan, quoting C. H. Knoblauch
> and Lil Brannon, *Cultural Reflections,* 1997

You see yourself when you see the Who.
> Pete Townshend of the Who

Understanding the cultural influences on the self is a central goal of many current English teachers, and since almost all writing can lead to self-discovery, writing is the premier English class method for devel-oping insight into one's self and one's culture. This chapter details how music can help teachers and students explore with writing and discussions who they are, how their identities have been culturally constituted, and how such awareness can lead them to be better read-ers and writers.

Analyzing Music to Understand Ourselves: Unmasking Racism

Marvin Gaye's smooth falsetto croons from the boom box. Occasionally a point I want to make with music requires playing two songs, in this case two different versions of Gaye's hit, "How Sweet It Is (To Be Loved by You)." That requirement raises some sticky practical issues. Do I start at the usual time and run farther into the official class period than I like to? Do I play pieces of both songs and hope students can get the point listening to just fragments? Or do I play the first song early, when few students will be around to hear it?

The latter approach would be particularly ironic with today's pair, which I play to get students thinking about where the opinions that they cherish as uniquely theirs really come from, how and why and by what they have been constructed. If I play Gaye's version first, most students—all but the early birds—hear only the second version, by Jerry Garcia's band, privileging the white cover version over the black original. It's exactly that privileging that I want to interrogate. I don't want to recapitulate the same unconscious bias that influenced the formative years of the construction of my own musical tastes. And I want students to see how analyzing such apparently minor decisions and choices can lead to important, perhaps unnerving, insights into ourselves and our worlds.

I didn't pay much attention to Gaye's song when it came out, though at the time I knew every song on A.M. radio's Top 40. It was late 1964, the Beatles were in the middle of a string of hits that left fans holding their breath for the next one, and the British Invasion had Eastern kids gazing longingly across the Atlantic for an early glimpse of the next Stones or Zombies. Some of us found it easy to take for granted music coming out of America's middle.

Besides, Marvin Gaye was Motown. Black music. Not something a white kid would listen to. I didn't feel a need for music from the other half of America. My allegiance had shifted, easily and smoothly, from the white crooners of the pre-Beatles era—Del Shannon and Bobby Vee and Roy Orbison—to the white British Invasion bands. Of course the Beatles and the Stones and later the blues bands on both sides of the Atlantic that became my next set of heroes—Paul Butterfield and the Blues Project and Cream—all owed their existence to black music and often, to their credit, said so. But it took me years to understand the full depth of that debt, the extent of the borrowing.

At the time, I didn't think of my dismissal of the heart of American music as racist. (Few people see the ugliness within, which is why this musical lesson is so important.) I'm not even sure

I consciously thought "Motown is black." But I knew, without think-ing about it much, and certainly without feeling anxious or guilty about it, that it wasn't my music. I can't blame my racist attitude on my fascination with British music. I had room in my collection for some Smokey Robinson or the Supremes. And I can't even claim media bias. Radio stations weren't as monochromatic as they'd been in the fifties. As I remember it, the Philadelphia A.M. stations I lis-tened to played roughly equal numbers of black and white artists—any station that played Gerry and the Pacemakers also played Wilson Pickett—and I don't remember the DJs making any invidious comparisons or slyly racist introductions, though of course it's pos-sible that they did.

No, I have only my twelve-year-old self to blame, which is to say, I was a product of a culture so thoroughly racist that it could produce subliminal racist musical reactions in a kid who lived in a world so white that he never had the opportunity to explore or question his own views on race. Working at a summer camp with a militant black radical when I was seventeen finally started me thinking about what civil rights might really mean and resulted in Huey Newton and Jimi Hendrix taking their place on my wall next to the Rolling Stones, but the process of identifying the racism in our reactions and decisions is a lifelong one, and in my case it needed (and still needs) all the help it can get.

Race didn't overtly enter my musical consciousness until I discov-ered Gaye's song eight years after it came out, when, as a college stu-dent, I taped a Jerry Garcia/Merl Saunders concert off the radio. When he wasn't on the road with the Grateful Dead or his bluegrass band, Old and In the Way, Garcia was playing in the Bay Area with what would later become known as the Jerry Garcia Band. The tape ended with a wonderful Motown tune that I knew from years before. Was it Smokey Robinson?

I liked the song enough to track down the original version, and when I listened to it and heard how good it was, I was forced to face the question of why I hadn't liked it eight years before. Long before I had heard the term, I began to analyze my own social constructedness.

Whenever I play this pair, I encourage students to think about their own tastes and where they might have come from and how they have been influenced. But I also have to admit to other motives that have less direct connection to the goals of English class. The realiza-tion about Gaye and Garcia eventually led me to what I now consid-er a central—and obvious—truth about Americans: that we are all, to some degree and at some level, racist, because our society is racist, and like it or not we are products of that society. I want students to consider, and perhaps accept, this generalization, because we can't help reduce the racism around us until we have seen, recognized, and acknowledged the racism within ourselves. Housecleaning has to begin within. I wouldn't point to a student's choices or taste and say "racist," but I have no trouble using the word with myself. And I know that at least some students follow my example.

As compelling as the insights of social construction are, they aren't necessarily easy to reveal to students. Racism is deeply ingrained in American culture, so anyone growing up in the culture can see it only when it is writ large and viewed from a sufficient distance. Students might apply the word to the dragging death of a black man, but they view the perpetrators of such acts as sickos, criminals, not representative of any significant segment of the general population, certainly not like them. Lincoln freed the slaves and the civil rights acts finished the job. Racism is dead.

So my first goal when talking about race is to bring racism home. We can look at a text and say, "Think about how Faulkner's South of the 1920s influenced his portrayal of black people in his novels." But most students, some emphatically, resist the idea that *they* are texts themselves, and that their views and behaviors might be to some degree determined by cultural forces. Nineteen-year-olds value their sense of free will above almost anything. So instead of challenging the students by asking them to analyze themselves, or asking them to analyze something they don't care about, I ask them to choose as a "text" for study something they're familiar with, even intimate with, and ask the question Why do I like this text?

Students are not as defensive about music as about politics or other personal choices and may see the value of asking the question, may be able to couch the issue in terms of influence rather than determinism, asking Who has meant a lot to me? rather than How have I been programmed? Most students can easily trace some aspects of their musical taste to their parents or friends, so it's not a big step to see larger forces at work in the formation of their taste.

In their book about using music in an interdisciplinary curriculum, Barrett, McCoy, and Veblen suggest a way to help students think systematically about the place of music in their lives. In their Circles exercise, they prompt students to ponder such things as "songs you recall singing in school," "recordings you would not want to live without," and "your least favorite musical examples," creating a "music circle" for each category. Then students examine how the circles relate, asking such questions as "In what ways do these circles reflect the influences of the time and place you were born, places you've lived, and significant people in your life?" (2).

Music in Our Lives

Each of the bulleted paragraphs below describes a way that music can affect us. Each can be turned into a question—e.g., Do you connect any songs with a specific moment?—for a freewrite, followed by a discussion of what our freewrites tell us about how music influences our views of reality.[1] Students like to tell stories about their experience with music, and though they may resist analysis, resist the notion that there's anything to analyze, it's pretty easy for a teacher to ask, Don't you think the violence on all those death metal album covers has an effect on you? Teachers wanting to raise these kinds of issues can share the stories in the paragraphs below or substitute their own. If students responded to the prompt at the beginning of Chapter 1, they may want to develop their own categories for "How music affects our lives."

■ Some songs are indelibly linked with a specific moment. Brendon was hooked for life on *A Love Supreme* because that's what he was listening to when he first made love. The Beatles' "Ask Me Why" has always been the song of triumph for me because I remember a moment I spent on our front walkway basking in the glory of a sixth-grade graduation award I'd just received, singing the song's unbelieving, ecstatic words. The musical association preserves that moment, keeps alive that award and that feeling, provides significant food for my malnourished ego. What clear evidence of the social construction of self: the song helped construct my sense of personal value.

■ Songs grab us because of idiosyncratic associations of words or phrases. One such association with a Poco song changed my life. After my sophomore year in college, I made a crucial decision under the influence of jet lag and airplane headphones as I flew east to spend a semester working apart from my girlfriend, Melody. Through the headphones came the best musical lineup I'd heard on an airplane, including Poco's "You'd Better Think Twice," from one of our favorite albums. In my sleep-deprived state, one line from that song—about being haunted by a melody—seemed written just for me and helped convince me to head back months earlier than planned. If that tune hadn't been so catchy, I might have stayed east for the semester, lost Melody, and lived out my life a heartbroken starving artist.

■ Music is handed down from parent to child, as much inheritance as a bald pate or a predisposition to teach. My seven-year-old daughter is already a Beatles and Sleater-Kinney fan.

■ Sometimes our culture forces songs into our consciousness, as if to prove the power of our social milieu to leave an impression on our brains and tastes. Even if we despise the song, we can't escape its influence. Every few months, someone beribbons trees to commemorate a loved one held hostage or prisoner, and yet another group of people learns from the execrable song "Tie a Yellow Ribbon 'Round the Ole Oak Tree" (Orlando) to turn desperate longing into cheesy public spectacle.

■ No doubt the most common connection between people and their music is that we identify particular music with particular relationships, and we learn the language, the mores, and the boundaries of relationships partly through songs. To what extent popular music influences our conception of relationships is a fascinating, though ultimately unanswerable question; I hope a twenty-first-century researcher replicates the kind of study of lyrics that Donald Horton wrote about in his 1957 article, "The Dialogue of Courtship in Popular Song." Many of Horton's conclusions seem as valid today as they were forty-five years ago—for example, that popular songs "offer the opportunity to experiment in imagination with the [sexual and relational] roles one will have to play in the future" (25). We're still debating, sometimes in Congress, the logical follow-up question: Do songs *influence* our sense of what roles we will play?

Music suggests how we begin relationships, how we feel when in love ("Shakin' All Over") (Johnny Kidd), what happens when the magic starts to run out ("I Used to Love Him") (Lauryn Hill), and what to wish on an estranged lover ("Burn, Don't Freeze!") (Sleater-Kinney). Does the song provoke the emotion, complicate it, clarify it, intensify it, provide catharsis, or merely articulate it? As a character asks in the opening scene of the movie *High Fidelity,* "Did I listen to pop music because I was miserable? Or was I miserable because I listened to pop music?" (quoted in Dettmar 2000b, B11). As Dettmar puts it, "Do our cultural narratives describe, or instead prescribe, our cultural and personal relationships?" (2000b, B11).

Far from being a new, postmodern worry, anxiety about how music fashions our view of relationships was raised by David Riesman in 1950: "Does the music tell these people, almost without their awareness, how to feel about their problems in much the same way that the daytime serials package their social lessons?" (9). Christenson and Roberts answer: "In the areas that cause the greatest public consternation, popular music and MTV probably reflect reality more than they create it" (12). But note the qualifiers they use. It's impossible to know how our concepts of gender and relationships might be different if they could be stripped of all influences from music, but it seems self-evident that to limit these effects, we need to make young people conscious of potential influences and discuss with them alternative gender roles and modes of relating.

Because of this recognition of music's complex relationship to our emotions and personal roles, students may be open to the idea that, for instance, "love at first sight" is a concept promoted by songs (and other pop culture), a potentially dangerous and perhaps artificial concept that might never occur to us if songs (and of course, films, short stories, and Shakespeare plays) didn't attune us to it. And if they can accept that a romantic concept that means so much to them was influenced, perhaps created, by a song, they're ready to swallow the central tenet of constructionism and perhaps begin to look for the social foundations of other concepts, tastes, and opinions that they consider theirs.

It seems likely that the emphasis in popular songs, the simple weight of thematic repetitions, affects our cultural sense of relational possibilities. Recently I faced the challenge of playing in class a piece of music that celebrated adult relationships and marriage, in honor of the wedding of a forty-something class member. I could offer dozens, perhaps hundreds, of songs about obsession and passion and relational imbalance—any kind of teenage emotion. And I could find a few adult characters and situations in the songs of great writers like Elvis Costello and Joni Mitchell. But celebration?

The best I could come up with was Talking Heads' "This Must Be the Place (Naive Melody)," in which David Byrne sings of the bliss of home and of a face with age and character (www.purelyrics .com/index.php?lyrics=gdnbsmdt). Why is it so hard to find songs about positive adult relationships? What might that difficulty say about our taste for, or perhaps the industry's production of heartache over contentment? Do the lovelorn buy more records than the happily mated? And why does Byrne undercut this rare positive song with the subtitle, "(Naive Melody)"? Is he saying that all positive feelings about adult relationships are naive?

■ Songs help us understand our world, the world beyond teenage relationships. Bob Dylan's "Masters of War" is an unsurpassed analysis of twentieth-century conflict; it gave many people their first insight into the influence of profit on global conflict and helped us understand one of the forces that kept us in Vietnam. Paul Simon's "Dangling Conversation" sheds light on a relationship in twilight, perhaps thirty years after the teenage excitement. Joni Mitchell's "Big Yellow Taxi" gave the environmental movement its best and most lasting image—the sacrifice of paradise for a parking lot (www.joni mitchell.com/Ladies70LyricsHome.html/).

Music and Change

Exploring the constructedness of self with music has an additional, unique advantage—we can do something about whatever we discover. Of course, on a national scale, racism seems intractable, and without the musical nudge, the rare student who opens her eyes wide enough to see racism generally feels content just recognizing its existence, naming it. One powerless person can't *do* anything about it.

But once we recognize the racism (and a host of other prejudices) within each of us, once analyzing music has shown us specific ways in which racism affects us and our worldview, we *can* do something about it. In my case, I can start listening to Marvin Gaye, lend a more sympathetic ear to other Motown artists, tell others about my discovery and encourage them to look for their own racism. Perhaps most important, having once seen the bias in my own opinions, I can be wary of making the same mistake again.

So, for instance, though I still can't get enthusiastic about most rap, I have managed to avoid the unthinking and often clearly racist judgments that many listeners, critics, and musicians make about it as a genre, and have begun finding rap that I enjoy. I encourage readers—especially those of my race and generation—to consciously open their ears to the rappers their students listen to and try to understand their appeal. After all, as Christenson and Roberts say, "rap is arguably the freshest, most compelling sound in contemporary popular music" (111). David Toop defends the genre's effects: "Not only did [hip-hop] help displace violence and the refuge of destructive drugs like heroin, but it also fostered an attitude of creating from limited materials" (15). As Houston Baker puts it, "you have to start with where they are." And where some students are is listening to rap. With Baker, I believe that "rap can be used to help students appreciate classic literature, ethics, philosophy, and other areas of study" (Waldron, 16). As rapper Chuck D put it, "Rap is the CNN of young black America" (Obstfeld and Fitzgerald, 39); if we're not "watching" it, we're out of touch. Yes, I'm still a cultural tourist in the world of rap, but at least I'm beginning to understand why some people want to live there.

Anyone who teaches a multiracial class needs to think about how important—how defining—hip-hop can be for some African Americans. I realize that the majority of the rap audience is white, and whites buy almost three quarters of rap records (Christenson and Roberts, 110). But it still seems likely that rap is more important as a locus of identity and expression for black than for white listeners. In one study of a middle school for "troubled" kids, 92 percent of the African American kids said rap was their favorite music, while 96 percent of their white peers chose heavy metal (Christenson and Roberts, 87). Such a musical divide can, I'm sure, create a chasm in the class, but I am convinced that teachers can also exploit such loyalties to bridge that chasm.

Expanding my tastes enough to listen to Motown and a bit of rap won't, of course, change the ossified economic, social, and political racism of our country. But any kind of widespread social change has to start with individuals. Whether presidents or just voters, people who deny the racism within can never truly contribute to any solution but will only compound the problem.

. . . And Gender

As my story about "Down by the River" demonstrates, music can help us change in tiny ways our treatment of gender as well as race. And while a discussion about *relationships* in popular music might turn giggly and silly, a more serious discussion of *gender roles* in music could lead to a whole unit on gender, maybe even a new understanding of the impact gender roles have in and to our lives.

For years, at least since Karen Durbin's 1974 article in *Ms.* magazine, "Can a Feminist Love the World's Greatest Rock and Roll Band?," people have been nervously asking themselves what their musical tastes say about their stance on gender issues. Can you dance to the Stones' "Stupid Girl" or "Under My Thumb," yet reject the attitudes that they seem to promote? What might the songs you listen to say about your own attitudes toward gender?

What do rap fans think, for instance, about what Richard Shusterman calls rap's "horribly macho celebrations of the (often violent) exploitation of women" (631)? I'm sure some would say they don't notice it, they're not aware of it, just as the juvenile attitudes toward women in much rock music go unremarked. Yet the relationship of gender consciousness to musical tastes is often clear to both me and my students. Most women who, by the age of eighteen or nineteen, have recognized the gender inequalities of our society have listened to at least some music—Alanis Morissette or Ani DiFranco or No Doubt—that questions, challenges, or rejects those inequalities. It's difficult to construct a convincing chain of cause and effect from such observations, but they leave me convinced that while feminist and postfeminist music might not be able to claim magical transformative powers, it clearly can play a role in sparking, articulating, and encouraging feminist thinking, while traditional misogynistic rock can do the opposite.

It would be easy to play and critique songs with archaic views of sex roles, but I prefer to let the songs themselves do the critiquing or to play examples of songs that break the mold and challenge the prevailing sexism. Arrested Development was the first rap group to break into my consciousness in part because of its apparent attitude toward women. The fully clothed women on the cover of their first album seem to have been selected for reasons other than to show off their bodies. And though "People Everyday" ends with a typically male scene of the hero fighting for the honor of "his" woman, I imagine most listeners also pick up on the song's respect toward the "black queen" and its point that commenting on a woman's "anatomy" is obnoxious.

As always, I'm on safest ground when I make myself the target of my critiques, and that's easy when gender is the issue. I don't usually plan out the sequence of music that I want to play over a month or a semester; I respond instead to the readings, activities, and discussions of each day as it comes. Sometimes I look back over the preceding weeks and realize that I've played music by men for five or six classes in a row. On the next day after such a realization, I'll play something by a woman—usually a PJ Harvey song that shoves gender issues into your face—and ask the class if they have noticed any patterns in my recent musical choices. Rarely, someone will say, "Yeah, they're all by men." More often, once I point out the maleness of my choices, students with a budding sense of gender awareness will shake their heads in disbelief that they didn't pick up on the pattern. They might have noticed it in the readings for other classes and been outraged, so how could they have missed it in this class?

That sense of frustration—at uncovering yet another area of blindness—is a good place to start a discussion. Why don't we notice? Does it matter that my music is so male, or that we accept its maleness without question? Why do I play so much male music? Am I justified in light of the fact that "from the earliest days of rock and roll at least 60 percent and at times as much as 75 percent of the top popular music performers have been male" (Christenson and Roberts, 126–27)? Male and female students *do* listen to different kinds of music and use music for different purposes, boys often to "pump themselves up," girls to "explore and cope with new concerns" (Christenson and Roberts, 52). Christenson and Roberts also cite a researcher who believes gender differences are so powerful in musical taste that all music should be divided simply into "male appeal" and "female appeal" (89). So I can't hide behind the excuse that all music is universal, and gender doesn't matter. John Shepherd asserts that "the vast majority of music consumed in the Western world is concerned with articulating, in a variety of different ways, male hegemonic processes" (171), and I believe he would argue that my musical tastes, from my preference for Janis Joplin over Joan Baez to the dominance of male performers in my music collection, reflect my typically male fear of and desire to control women as fertile nurturers.

Everywhere around me I see gender bias in popular music and especially rock: my 1232-page *All Music Guide to Rock* (Hodges et al.) lists five editors, all of them male, and out of 105 contributors, only nine are clearly female. Why should that matter? In the construction of our tastes, gender is inevitably a major factor. A male critic will see Madonna and Tori Amos and the Backstreet Boys—and to a lesser extent all performers—differently from a female critic. Not better or worse, more or less accurately, but differently. And if most of the eyes doing the seeing are male, much of the value of female vision may be unavailable to readers.

The gender bias in the music I play for class provides a focal point for discussing either the deterministic details of social construction or the values and dangers of affirmative action. Gender studies courses might ask questions like the following of written texts or the weighty actions of politicians, creating classes in which the personal stakes and tensions could be high. Asking them about my musical selections for class means that the stakes are low, the chance for insult small, and that we all share the same concrete information to refer to.

- Can I escape the social influences of my upbringing? What if I played lots of music by black women—would that simply further affirm the power of personal background?
- What in the way rock musicians are valued and marketed makes it easier for male rockers to impress me than for women?
- How would substituting a female voice for a male voice in my class music selections change the class?
- Can I excuse my apparent gender bias by pointing out that rock music is marketed for the young and that "youth cultures and subcultures tend to be some form of exploration of masculinity" (Mike Brake quoted in Straw, 104)?
- Is it legitimate to quote Christenson and Roberts—"girls listen more than boys, at least once adolescence is reached" (38)—and argue that I need male music to get the attention of male students, the ones most likely to be mentally wandering?
- How can I keep from creating an atmosphere that would lead women students to do, metaphorically, what one of Christenson and Roberts' students did literally—put her Madonna album on a tape labeled "The Doors" (86)?
- How should I select tomorrow's music—should I continue to look for the perfect song in my collection, as I usually do, or should I pay particular attention to the women musicians I can think of?

For those who say "To hell with affirmative action, play the best song!" I have a story. I once noticed that I'd been playing mostly men, and decided to do something about it, just days before I planned to talk about lyrics and poetry. As I discuss in Chapter 7, I think ultimately the question Could these song lyrics be considered poetry? is silly and condescending, but even to make that point, I like to have students think about a relatively poetic song. Bob Dylan's songs are the obvious choice, especially since Andrew Motion, the poet laureate of Great Britain, declared in 2000 that Dylan was "one of the greatest artists of the century" and "Visions of Johanna" "the best song lyric ever written" (Kelley).

But, to fill my affirmative action quota, I needed a woman. Joni Mitchell and her song "Both Sides Now" leapt to mind (www.jonimitchell.com/jonihome.html#Lyrics). At first I thought that Mitchell's song couldn't stand up next to anything Dylan was doing in the sixties. But as I examined—interviewed, you might say—the song, I began to realize in how many ways it was an excellent choice. The images of clouds are self-consciously poetic, the phrases carefully turned, while the subject of the song itself is writing, poetry, the triumph of illusion, the changing of perspective, the doubleness of everything in the mind of a self-conscious writer. It is indeed a great song, a fine piece of writing. And I might never have made that discovery if I hadn't done a little affirmative action on my own tastes.

After playing Joni Mitchell and articulating my worries about my own gender bias and my own affirmative action principles, I can take the class in many different directions, depending on the course. In an English education course, I would make the point on a day when we were discussing something by Deborah Tannen about gender, communication, and classroom dynamics. I would use the students' blindness to the gender bias in my music to persuade them that they may not be as alert to such bias in classroom discussions as they had imagined. Then we would venture into the tricky, fascinating, and for teachers crucial area of male domination of classroom discussions. Do men really talk more in class, interrupt more, get away with more?

In a composition class, I might turn students lose on an old favorite prompt: imagine you woke up one morning as the opposite sex. How would your life and outlook be different? What would you think and feel? Or I might ask them to search their own experience for instances of affirmative action. How do they choose friends, or teammates for a pickup basketball game, or people to work with them on the yearbook? Does the "most qualified" person always get the nod?

I might pursue a similar strategy in a literature class, asking students to ponder the results of some noncanonical affirmative action that they or their teachers might have taken in choosing books to read. Have they ever started to read a book not because they thought it was great but because it would impress someone, or the teacher insisted there had to be a black woman author on the list, or they felt dumb because they'd never read anything by a Hispanic author? How did such affirmative action work out, and would they repeat the experiment?

. . . In Taste and Judgment

Not all the biases that music can reveal are as weighty as those concerning race and gender. But even musical leanings that have nothing to do with lyrics can teach us how much past and present social pressures and biases influence our present tastes. Our desire to be cool can limit our tastes and pressure us to conform and be critical, because, as Riesman points out, "enthusiasm would seem to be a greater social danger than negativism: the fear is to be caught liking what the others have decided not to like" (12). Arguing about tastes is self-defeating; as Anthony DeCurtis puts it, "What is the point . . . of pitting one type of music, or one work of art, or one type of knowledge against another, as if in a popularity contest?" (258). If someone can help me develop enthusiasm about a musician or an author I had previously scorned, suddenly the range of things that give me pleasure is wider. That has to be a good thing.

So what's to be done about critical judgment and evaluation? Do we abandon it entirely in discussing music—or writing? I no longer see the value of criticizing or even comparing most music. I can't talk you out of something you like, and I'm not sure I would want to, even if I could. But I *can* see the value of listening to your enthusiasm and hoping it's contagious. Explaining your enthusiasm takes critical thinking in the broader sense, thinking that focuses on critical elements of a work and connects specifics to generalizations in a way that helps me see. I don't want to *improve* tastes—my own or my students'—but I do want to *broaden* them.

As a writing teacher, I seldom have trouble distinguishing between good and better papers or finding ways in which individual writers or papers could improve. But my familiarity with music makes me wary of absolute judgments. Every musical "mistake" I can think of—from feedback to studio talk caught on tape to dead air to scratched records—has been incorporated into something considered music, just as writers have used nonstandard grammar enough that it constitutes a whole different way of making sentences, what Winston Weathers calls Grammar B.

The existence of Grammar B and of musical "mistakes" on record does not mean that in either music or writing, anything goes, any time. Instead, it should lead to a valuable discussion of how purpose, audience, genre, form, and format determine appropriateness. I doubt even the most ardent hip-hop fans would argue for incorporating record scratching and sampling in a performance of Mozart. And they would be outraged if someone insisted that every pop recording follow the organizational principles of a concerto or symphony. With the external elements of writing—purpose, audience, genre—known or chosen, the writer can more easily determine how to make other, smaller writing decisions.

. . . And Expanding Horizons

As a reader/listener, I try no longer to divide the universe into "like"/"dislike" or "good"/"bad" but "like"/"don't yet appreciate" or "good"/"good in some way I don't yet understand." And instead of arming my students with critical tools to help them reveal the weaknesses of a particular text, I try—in class and throughout this book—to suggest and model ways that they can expand their listening and reading horizons and at least glimpse the strengths that others see or hear.

I tell many stories about expanding my tastes because I think this issue is important, and I know that some students pick up on the idea and imitate me, listening to different kinds of music, trying to keep an open mind. Some seem to have made up their minds and cemented their tastes, but I hold on to the hope that college is a time of change and, as Christenson and Roberts put it, "periods of change are periods of uncertainty, and uncertainty leads to information seeking" (27).

Many of my students accept my invitation to expose me to new music to help me overcome my own limitations and prejudices. One such prejudice that I readily acknowledge is my predilection for real instruments played by real people. Synthesizers and space noises generally leave me cold. Drum machines make me hunger for flailing wood on skin. A computer could never imitate the sounds of strings, reeds, brass, or wood.

But the enthusiasm of AJ, a student in my Stranded class, opened my mind to exceptions. (Those of us over thirty years old must, I think, rely on our students and our own kids to keep us from becoming dinosaurs; even the veteran record executives who first signed hip-hop artists had to "follow their children," as Toop puts it [17].) Having plumbed my musical tastes, AJ was certain that I would like Nine Inch Nails despite its inhuman, techno-industrial sound. He lent me NIИ's first CD, *Pretty Hate Machine*, and told me to listen to

"Sanctified," loud. I did, and I was hooked. The most forceful sound in the song, both a release and an increase of pressure, has the decidedly noninstrumental timber of a steam valve being opened. But it works. And because I sought out and welcomed something outside of the sounds approved by my background, I discovered another source of creative and aesthetic pleasure. Keeping our minds open about musical tastes may help us accept diversity wherever we see it.

The Positive Side of Musical Analysis

Although musical analysis can be overly critical and reveal the dark side of humanity, it can highlight the positive as well. Students love to write papers about music's universal qualities, its ubiquitousness, its cross-generational appeal. Such papers are often not as interesting (for me, anyway) as ones that reach more concrete conclusions, but they're a step toward getting students to think across the boundaries of age, gender, and culture, and that step is in turn necessary for students to start to assess the cultural importance of those boundaries.

A student's interest in music often allows me to see positive aspects of that student that would otherwise be obscured by a bad attitude, poor grades, or a tough demeanor. Richie had long black hair and wore a leather jacket with concert T-shirts of what I learned were "death metal" bands. The clean-cut, froth-rock kids in class gave him a wide berth, and in the first week of class, he opened his mouth only to make caustic comments. But when I got a chance to ask him about death metal, he was as enthusiastic and childlike as a ten-year-old raving about his favorite sports team, and he displayed a surprisingly philosophical attitude about his favorite music, emphasizing the emotional power and necessity of staring at the eye sockets of the skull and laughing.

Kate Snyder's "The Green Pillows" (Appendix B) is a fine example of the kind of understanding a writer can reach by digging into the reasons behind musical taste. Her musical analysis didn't so much lead her to surprising insights as help her to see and link her own needs and strengths. You could read the entire paper without seeing that music was the catalyst, the conduit, the spark that started the blaze. And that's just fine. I'm not so much interested in having students write *about* music as I am in having them write with or because of or in response to music.

Despite the positive potential of the kind of analysis I've been discussing, many people resist the social constructionist perspective in part because, if taken to an extreme, it could lead to the conclusion that all taste, and perhaps all creative output, is predictable, determined by the social forces that make us up. Sometimes it seems as though the goal of constructionist analysis is a computer program into which we could feed all of our individual data, and out would come everything we've ever written or said.

To combat this feeling of creative determinism, I like to make sure that we don't pretend to have eliminated the mysterious, the unknowable, the impossibly complex from our approach to reading texts and understanding ourselves. While I think we can analyze fairly accurately the constituents of taste, and Christenson and Roberts assert that "one can predict music preference with some accuracy based on a mere handful of demographic and background variables" (80), that's not the same as being able to say with confidence why a certain song appeals to a certain person.

Sometimes I weave a web of convincing intellectual justifications for why I've fallen in love with a song, then part of me will rebel and say, I like it because I like the sound of her voice when she sings "God Is a Number" (Sleater-Kinney). Taking a constructionist stance doesn't reduce the mystery of taste; it just gives us interesting ways to probe that mystery, interesting questions to ask.

Write: Beyond the Individual

The first time I ask my students to analyze the song they chose at the beginning of the period, I have them look for personal connections (Chapter 1). The second time, I ask them to look for social or cultural factors that might have influenced their interest in a particular song. Did they, as I did, tacitly divide music along racial lines? Is the music they like specific to their generation? How does such generational identification with music occur? Did anyone in their school or family turn them on to the song? What other social questions are relevant to their selection?

I have students brainstorm answers to these questions for a few minutes, then search their writing about the song for assumptions, those embedded, culturally influenced beliefs that are crucial to our view of the world, yet often invisible to us. Do they assume, for instance, that lyrics—at least some lyrics—are Truth and can help listeners make decisions and understand their lives? Do they assume a different standard for music than for other forms of writing, accepting rhymes, clichés, and weak analogies that they wouldn't accept in poetry? Are they drawn to the music initially because some person or group—parental, social, religious—labeled it unacceptable?

This writing activity leads naturally into those that open and close Chapter 4, in which students articulate, make specific, and analyze their gut reactions to music and literature. Having examined some of the assumptions and biases that influence their gut, students can more readily move between the analytical and the nonanalytical, the intuitive and the critical, with an understanding that their reactions are subjective, influenced by myriads of background factors, yet nonetheless important.

Note

1. Anyone who wants more suggestions can consult Christenson and Roberts, who list thirty-four items in their table, A Partial Inventory of Popular Music Uses and Gratifications (42), and provide detailed explanations of their five main categories of "uses and gratifications"—cognition, diversion, social utili ty, withdrawal, and personal identity (43–44).

Three

Creating Contexts

Music is a window to thought and feeling, history and culture, the individual and society.
Janet R. Barrett, Claire W. McCoy, and Kari K. Veblen,
Sound Ways of Knowing, 1997

I was an angry teenager in a small Midwestern town, and a band like the Clash was giving me a much more accurate portrayal of U.S. foreign policy in Central America than Dan Rather was.
Rage Against the Machine guitarist Tom Morello, 1999

Context *has dominated the world of literary theory since New Criticism got old. Each new wave of theory has asserted that a text should be examined in a different context—structural, economic, historical, feminist, psychological, biographical, relational, cultural. The central question of social constructionism could be framed as Out of what contexts did this text grow? Before passing any judgment, postmodern thinkers ask, In what context? Cultural studies is particularly insistent that among the most important of those contexts are politics and "historical specificity."*

Defining context and showing how it affects meaning are, therefore, two crucial jobs for the modern English teacher. Music, of course, can help.

Establishing a Class Context

Choosing music for the first class of the semester is a complex business: what kind of tone, atmosphere, environment, and context do I want to create to introduce students to writing, working together, and my class? Sometimes I play one of my own creations, figuring if I act silly and make myself vulnerable the first day, I'll set a tone for self-disclosure and participation. I often start literature classes with the Smiths' "Cemetry Gates," with its image of the literary snob who always knows better than you and laughs at your failures. "We're not going to let that snob in the classroom," I proclaim, and a couple of students grin.

But more often, first days are so hectic and student attention so scattered that I play something just to soothe or amuse. If it's before noon, I often pick the Beatles' "Good Morning, Good Morning." It's lively and cheerful, especially if you don't look too closely at the words, and though it wouldn't be on my Top-50 list of Beatles songs, it does a fair job of representing me and my tastes. Seeing the obvious link between the song and the class can encourage students to listen closely and think about connections whenever I play music.

Defining and Appreciating Contexts

With Blues

Although the cultural gap that separates me from my students widens with the growing difference in our ages, we do have some musical favorites in common. For instance, many of my students are fond of that mellow old singer, Eric Clapton. I find Clapton's evolution into a vocalist ironic, because I know him as the blues guitar wiz who inspired "Clapton Is God" graffiti when playing with the Yardbirds, John Mayall, Cream, and Blind Faith in the 1960s. In those days, rumor had it that Clapton was not impressed with his own voice and had to be talked into heading for the microphone. Keith and John and Jack and Steve were singers; Eric was the guitarist.

But as early as 1968, he was singing at least one song on stage, "Crossroads," still one of his signature songs. Students often know the song, since a different group records a cover version of it every few years, and many have also seen the Walter Hill movie of the same title. Clapton's supergroup Cream put a live version of it on their album *Wheels of Fire*, but it wasn't Clapton's singing—or the barely intelligible and seemingly random lyrics—that fans listened for. Clapton's energetic guitar lines and his interplay with bassist Jack

Bruce still define white blues players' most significant contribution to their genre—the extended instrumental jam that owed much to jazz and in turn influenced the development of fusion.

But what does the song mean, what is its significance, what do the lyrics add up to? In 1967, *Time* magazine asserted that Cream's motto was "Forget the message, forget the lyrics; just play," a sentiment shared by many rock musicians then and now ("Forget the message"). Like, I would assume, most Clapton fans, I couldn't have told you, when I first listened to Cream, what the song was about. I could repeat, even sing, individual phrases, but without lyric sheets—a rarity in those days—the best I could do was conjure a vague image of someone hitchhiking at an intersection . . . until I did a little historical research and some thinking about contexts.

Even without any outside knowledge, a listener can put "Crossroads" in several contexts—Eric Clapton's music and his development as a guitarist and a singer, the evolution of blues guitar into rock guitar and of the blues as a genre into rock, the meaning(lessness) of rock lyrics. Anyone who read the record label or listened to Clapton talk about the song knew that it was written by someone named Robert Johnson, and a little investigation reveals that Johnson recorded two takes of "Cross Road Blues" in 1936. Close listening to Johnson's version helps explain the problems with Clapton's lyrics—one whole verse of the Cream version doesn't appear in Johnson's "Cross Road" but in another Johnson tune, "Traveling Riverside Blues." (And, Clapton says, "the riff for [his version of the song] came more or less from 'Terraplane,'" a third Johnson song [Guralnick, 47].)

Placing the two versions side by side suggests more contexts that could illuminate the song—the shifts in the blues from acoustic and rural to electric and urban (and from poor Southern black American to white British working class), the borrowings of white musicians and what they owe African Americans, the relationship of blues to jazz (Johnson's music shows up in jazz histories like the Smithsonian jazz collection), Depression-era music, southern music . . . the list is almost endless.

But for me the most interesting—most chilling—meaning of the lyrics doesn't arise until they are put in the context of southern rural life in the 1930s. Historical specificity is crucial, and I'm sure historians of Southern black culture could tease out many layers of meaning in the song. For a black man in that place and time, "dark gonna catch me here" could be not just inconvenient, but terrifying. The singer wants someone to run get his friend Willie Brown not because he's lazy but because his life could be in danger. Especially in light of the legend that

Robert Johnson's genius derived from a devil's bargain, the fact that the singer is at the crossroads, a traditional place to meet the devil, is even more ominous. The emotion, the expression in Clapton's version comes through the guitar. In Johnson's version, it's in the singing and the lyrics; we follow the singer from the rejection of "everybody pass me by" to the fear of darkness approaching, to the vocal strain in the final verse on the repeated word "run." In the end, when Johnson laments, "I believe I'm sinkin' down," we sink with him.

This demonstration of the value and importance of context and historical antecedents can broaden and deepen student thinking during the early stages of work on a research paper. I ask students to come to class with a research subject in their heads, then think of any historical precursors to their subject that might shed light on it. Someone writing about drug legalization might look at Prohibition or the Congressional debates that led to drug bans. A student exploring natural childbirth might ponder childbirth in Colonial America, when "natural" was the only choice. A student interested in the "new" genre of creative nonfiction might ask what kinds of nonfiction were being written before the 1960s and new journalism. We often encourage our students to find up-to-date sources, but it may be just as important for them to learn some of the history out of which their subject emerged.

The writing exercise at the end of this chapter suggests another way to use this example—have students choose a detail from their subject and write about it in very specific terms, then have them brainstorm as many contexts as possible in which the detail might be meaningful. (I leave my list of contexts for "Cross Roads" on the board to spur students to move beyond the obvious.) I like to hear from as many students as possible after such an exercise, to help them explore imaginatively the papers they might write if they placed their subjects in the various different contexts.

With Relationships

Probably the easiest subject for students to analyze on their own, with their own examples, is love. Every day brings new love songs to the radio, and everyone knows at least a few, so they can productively ask

- What is the context that this song creates for relationships?
- What are the assumptions and beliefs behind it, what facts or events or feelings does it emphasize or ignore?
- Does the song, like "Ball and Chain" (Big Brother), focus on the unhealthy, addictive aspects of love?

- Does it blur the line between love and sex ("Let's Get It On" [Gaye]) or trivialize relationships in general?
- Does it leave open the possibility of homosexual love?
- Does it, like the Hollies' song "Just One Look," promote the concept of love at first sight?
- Does it construct a vision of long-term, adult love? (See Chapter 2.)

Students have no problem finding a love song, and if they're not too immersed in living out that song at the moment, they can see that the worldview implied by their song is different from that of "Sanctified" by Nine Inch Nails or *A Love Supreme* by John Coltrane. What is it about the Cure's mopey dark desperation that attracts one student while Britney Spears' dance tunes entrance another? How did they come to have such tastes, such visions of relationships? Do friends react with "cool" to one version of love and deride the others? How does the culture respond to the song's excesses? Who profits from their successes? What metaphors for love are floating in students' heads, love as a "buzz" (Nirvana) or a "four-letter word" (Baez)?

With "The Facets Model"

Teachers looking for a set of context questions to use methodically might check out the Facets Model for Studying Artistic Works (Barrett, McCoy, and Veblen, 76–77). In this model, "the Work" sits at the center, with eight questions providing the facets:

- Who created it?
- When and where was it created?
- Why and for whom was it created?
- What does it sound or look like?
- What kind of structure or form does it have?
- What is its subject?
- What is being expressed?
- What techniques did its creator use to help us understand what is being expressed?

Whether the questions are systematically or intuitively linked, the goal is the same—to move beyond first impressions and start making connections, seeing bigger pictures, appreciating how profoundly context determines meaning.

Providing Context

To reach these goals, many teachers have long used music primarily as a cultural artifact, something mentioned in, or that illuminates, a text.

Some texts demand musical accompaniment. James Baldwin's much-anthologized short story "Sonny's Blues," for instance, uses a musical rift—between Louis Armstrong and Charlie Parker—to explain how the two brothers are pulling apart, and Sonny's hard-earned moment of personal triumph comes when he's playing "Am I Blue?," a song Billie Holiday immortalized. I leap at the chance to play music by any of these three jazz giants since they're usually little more than names to current students. The music can help students get it—the difference in the styles, the importance of the musicians—in a way that nothing else can. Listening to a minute or so of Louis Armstrong's melodic, rhythmic trumpet, then switching to the frenetic hard bop of Charlie Parker explains better than anything else why the two brothers are at odds over nothing and everything, why someone who thinks of jazz as Armstrong can't understand the world of someone who idolizes Parker.

Music can also furnish the sound or flavor of particular eras, which is useful for setting the cultural and sensory scene for literature, history, social studies, art history, or sociology. Work songs of various eras contribute a sense of what life was like outside of the juke joints and bedrooms on which much music focuses. Taj Mahal—a historian of traditional music as well as a performer—records songs like "Linin' Track" to help us imagine what backbreaking construction work was like before the era of backhoes. Songs like "The Erie Canal" keep alive the work environments of the nineteenth century, and on-site recordings made since the 1930s help us imagine both a particular moment in history and moments that preceded it, often reaching back to the dark days of slavery. Many of Alan Lomax's recordings of work songs, calls, and prison songs remind pampered listeners that outside of the world of Disney, singing while you work can be more a matter of survival than of joy.

Those songs and the spirituals that often accompanied them provide a way to connect with slave life, a life that, for better or worse, American students today have difficulty imagining. Think of "Go Down Moses," the passion of the plea for a great leader, someone to stand up to the Pharaoh, the determination of the repeated demand "let my people go." The song uses one people's trouble to talk about another's, thus encouraging listeners to extend the analogy or make a similar one. The analogy of Jews to slaves, Pharaoh to President or Master, invites today's listeners and singers to identify with oppressed peoples through the ages, which is surely a good thing.

Songs can provide context and empathy for almost any minority group or activity. Patti Smith's "Ghost Dance," for instance, can spark discussions of cultural appropriation, treatment of the sacred, and of course the genocide of Native Americans. In "Babelogue," Smith alludes to being a Comanche, but I doubt that helps her imagine what the ghost dances sounded like as desperate Western Indians searched for an alternative to annihilation. I have no idea if Smith's song resembles the chants of 1889 and 1890, but it does give current audiences a quick primer in the ghost dance craze. It sounds like a dirge, with only the thinnest thread of hope, yet it's possible to imagine dancing to it for hours. Is it blasphemous to pretend to re-create the death dance of a people? Is Smith profiting from the tragedy, or is she doing an important service by telling the native story to the world? Is this cultural appropriation or cultural appreciation?

We need Cab Calloway and Bessie Smith to evoke the roaring twenties, the West Coast Pop Art Experimental Band's "A Child of a Few Hours Is Burning to Death" to recall the horror with which sensate people reacted to Vietnam, George M. Cohan's "Over There" to get a taste of what the First World War years sounded like back home, Holly Near and Ronnie Gilbert's impassioned "Biko" to open a discussion of Apartheid and American complicity in it. We can follow the black migration from the south to Chicago by tracing a song from Robert Johnson to Muddy Waters to Buddy Guy. We can introduce a central image in African American life by playing the 1996 Fugees' song, "The Mask," then giving out copies of Paul Laurence Dunbar's 1896 poem "We Wear the Mask" and perhaps going on a hunt for other mask references in Frederick Douglass or Sojourner Truth (see Chapter 4).

We invoke the carefree feeling of the pre–JFK assassination world by playing the Beach Boys' surf songs or early "girl groups." We enliven a discussion of the McCarthy years by playing Dylan's "Talkin' John Birch Paranoid Blues," a song that was pulled from the *Freewheelin' Bob Dylan* album and that CBS refused, at the last minute, to let Dylan play on the *Ed Sullivan Show,* causing Dylan to walk out and never play on the top entertainment show of the era.

To discuss the evolution of the modern women's movement, we can sketch a number of musical progressions, from "Johnny Get Angry," whose female narrator wants to be lectured by her Neanderthal boyfriend (Joanie Sommers) or "He Hit Me (and It Felt Like a Kiss)" (Crystals) through Janis Joplin's "Women Is Losers" (Big Brother) to Insect Trust's "Declaration of Independence" or Peggy Seeger's "I'm Gonna Be an Engineer" (see Figure 6–1), Patti Smith's

"Gloria" (see Chapter 1), or any number of songs by PJ Harvey, Liz Phair, or Ani DiFranco.

To call to mind the Me generation of the 1980s, we can start with Bobby McFerrin's "Don't Worry, Be Happy," and to show the kind of reaction that era produced, we can play a song by Minor Threat, founders of the straight-edge movement, sober, straight, and tired of apathy: "You tell me that I make no difference / At least I'm fuckin' trying / What the fuck have you done?" ("In My Eyes"). We play Billie Holiday's "Strange Fruit" for students who think that racism ended with slavery, reminding them that no president until Franklin Roosevelt (on 12/6/33) made a "straightforward denunciation of lynching" (Wilson, 162).

Though he has recorded almost nothing since the 1960s ("Political satire became obsolete when Henry Kissinger was awarded the [1973] Nobel [Peace] prize" [Thompson]), Tom Lehrer is still, to my mind, the leading musical commentator of modern American life, and his songs provide a particularly useful reflection of world social and political events in the 1950s and sixties. Lehrer's "Oedipus Rex" (promotional song for an imagined movie of the Sophocles play) leads students, laughing, into the weighty world of Greek tragedy and Freudian psychology. His "New Math" offers an eternal theme song for educational fads: "It's so simple / so very simple / that only a child can do it." "Who's Next" and "We Will All Go Together When We Go" describe the insane, childish, but very real world of nuclear proliferation and annihilation, and their humor helps put the horror at a distance ("We'll all fry together when we fry"). He takes jabs at hunters, Boy Scouts, the South, the West, the Irish, hometown hypocrisy, the army, and romance. His exaggeration is never far removed from what we think of as the truth, and people susceptible to his message will find him consistently wise.

Lehrer's "Pollution" is typical of his many songs that can rearrange the listener's thinking (see Figure 3–1). He begins the song in a mock Mexican accent, presenting advice to foreigners about going to American cities: "Don't drink the water and don't breathe the air." The reversal of the typical U.S. warning about the south-of-the-border dangers of Montezuma's revenge is brilliant, quick, and catchy— listeners who get the tune in their head will find it difficult ever after to think with condescension about other countries' health dangers. The mock Mexican accent can also open up a discussion of when humor becomes offensive, when satire becomes mockery, when caricature becomes racism.

When provided with a little context, students can also learn from the song to complicate their definition of environmentalism.

New "greens" often take pride in their generation's having opened the world's eyes to environmental problems, and true idealists think that we will soon solve them. Both may be surprised and chastened to learn that Lehrer's song came out in 1965, five years before the first Earth Day. And many anti-environmentalists may feel that they've never before run into an environmentalist with a sense of humor.

Lehrer even captures some of the political complexity of the issue in his last verse, when he notes in the live version of the song, recorded in San Francisco, that "the breakfast garbage that you throw into the bay / They drink at lunch in San Jose." Almost two generations later, we haven't yet learned the simple lesson of this line: dumping our problem just makes it someone else's problem. Lehrer's song seems to mock those who think if they can just overcome "ignorance" by broadcasting their messages in clever ways, they can reverse the trend. It carries the depressing implication that even a clever, witty, insightful, factual exposé is unlikely to change anything.

Create Your Own Context: "Jukebox for the 1990s"

In their music-oriented lesson-plan collection, *Row, Row, Row Your Class*, Dawn DiPrince and colleagues suggest a class exercise that involves students in *creating* context, not just identifying or using it. It asks students to define their own era, create the musical soundtrack of their time, become active agents in the process of social construction, in defining how they will be perceived. If we are to steep students in the insights of social construction, it is important to demonstrate that they don't have to see themselves as passive victims of someone else's construct; they can sometimes control the process.

The directions for "Jukebox for the 1990s" begin, "Suppose that you could preserve five songs in a modern jukebox for your grandchildren to discover 50 years from now. What five songs would you choose? Why?" Students who have had some experience thinking of other times and places in terms of their music may have some notion of the complexity of constructing their era with five musical choices. "Do you want to include . . . songs you are pretty sure will sound silly to your grandchildren?" *Row*'s authors ask (10). Is the image we want future generations to construct of us an image that includes silliness?

This activity could lead to a discussion of the many kinds of control that the individual writer and reader exercise. Every piece we write creates its own world, its own idealized audience, our own versions of reality and truth.

Write: Close-Ups and Contexts

A crucial part of many writing processes is adjusting, experimenting with, making best use of distance. I don't know what I would do without camera metaphors, but because all my students are familiar with a camera's ability to provide the big picture—all of North America from the space station—or zoom in on the pistil and stamen of a rare orchid in Minnesota, they easily understand how a photographer or a movie director can vary the distance to the subject. Analysis of songs can provide a bridge between such an understanding of visual distance and the zoom-lens techniques that writers use. Students can see, for instance, that in Tom Lehrer's "Pollution," "The breakfast garbage that you throw into the Bay" is a close-up, a detail you can smell if you think about it, whereas the title provides one big picture, one context, and, as I mentioned above, U.S.–Mexican relations provides another.

To help students apply this zoom lens to their own writing, I ask them to get a subject in mind and, first, write a paragraph—scene, dialogue, description, stream-of-consciousness—to get as close to that subject as possible, showing us the subject as it moves, breathes, thinks, and is licked by the dawn's early light.

Besides taking examples from the Lehrer song, I ask students to think about newspaper and magazine stories and how they vary distance, closing in on an individual person or event to provoke interest—we see Jane Doe, twenty-two-year-old single mother of two, living on beans and ketchup. But the article also backs away from Jane Doe, creating distance, perspective, asking readers to see her in the context of welfare reform or poverty in America or alimony laws or American dietary problems. Without the close-up, the story is likely to lack interest; without the distance, it lacks meaning and significance.

So after they've spent some time on the close-up, students brainstorm as many contexts as possible in which their close-up might be meaningful. This is a difficult step for some students, so I always model what I mean. If I've just written a scene of college drinking as my close-up, I'll jot down on the board a dozen or so contexts in which that scene would have meaning—higher education, America's drug problem, coming-of-age rituals, the Greek system on campuses, teaching college students, the current youth culture, diseases and social pathologies of young people, date rape, eating disorders, parental fears.

Finally, they write a paragraph in which they begin to connect the detail to the context and to probe that connection for significance and meaning. Linking the drinking scene and America's drug problem, for instance, might lead to an interesting discussion about how much we're influenced by media representations of certain behaviors: we're programmed to see the drinking scene as a healthy, even therapeutic part of American life, while TV portrays illegal drugs with images of junkies shaking in the bathroom, eggs frying. You'd never guess from those images that alcohol kills scores of times more people than do all illegal drugs combined.

This process of developing meaning by putting a single detail into context is fundamental to most student literature papers, but it is also a good way to approach almost any kind of writing assignment.

Figure 3–1

Pollution

1. If you visit American city,
You will find it very pretty
Just two things of which you must beware
Don't drink the water and don't breathe the air.

Pollution, Pollution,
They got smog and sewage and mud,
Turn on your tap and get hot and cold running crud.

2. See the halibuts and the sturgeons
Being wiped out by detergents.
Fish gotta swim and birds gotta fly,
But they don't last long if they try.

Pollution, Pollution,
You can use the latest toothpaste,
And then rinse your mouth with industrial waste.

3. Just go out for a breath of air,
And you'll be ready for Medicare,
The city streets are really quite a thrill,
If the hoods don't get you, the monoxide will.

Pollution, Pollution,
Wear a gas mask and a veil,
Then you can breathe, long as you don't inhale.

4. Lots of things there that you can drink,
But stay away from the kitchen sink,
Throw out your breakfast garbage, and I've got a hunch
That the folks downstream will drink it for lunch.

So go to the city, see the crazy people there.
Like lambs to the slaughter,
They're drinking the water
And breathing (*cough* ...) the air.

Four

Understanding Interpretation

Interpreting a message is as much a process of construction as discovery. The meaning of any message derives from both the content of the message and the experiences and expectations people carry around inside their heads.
        Peter G. Christenson and Donald F. Roberts,
                It's Not Only Rock & Roll, 1998

Every English class involves interpretation, *whether or not we use that word. Understanding and discussing how and why we read and respond to texts as we do can help students see the validity and value of interpretations in a new light, learn to trust and explore their own reactions, and begin to make their own interpretations convincing by referring to textual evidence. Everyone interprets music, and in this chapter we begin to examine how we can use students' interest in understanding music to spark discussions about key issues of interpretation and meaning.*

Where It All Starts

For once, I speak before I push play. "I want you just to listen and react, maybe jot something down. I'm looking for first impressions. Nothing analytical."

"Don't eat it," Jon Clark's voice strains from the CD player. "You don't need it / it's fat and sugar / chocolate butter / lies lies lies lies. / Fudge bar / you are / the best by far" (Sinkhole).

Music can quickly provide an experience that is both familiar—everyone has listened to music—and new. Teachers have no trouble coming up with songs that no student will have heard, whether they're by Chopin, Paul Simon, or Snoop Doggy Dogg. That combination of familiar and new is particularly useful when I want to get students thinking about how they react to a first "reading." I want them to see *interpretation* and *meaning* in a new light. I'm concerned that many students jump immediately to questions of point, message, or significance, ignoring the perhaps more important and certainly preceding step of reacting viscerally, emotionally, idiosyncratically, with associations that come from their upbringing, their schooling, their reading and listening. I'm convinced that even most scholarly writing about art starts with an inchoate, visceral, personal reaction that might be voiced "yeah" or "I don't get the appeal" or "yuck" or "hmmm, what have we here?" Gardner argues that even the insights of "logical-mathematical intelligence" are often nonverbal: "A solution to a problem can be constructed *before* it is articulated" (20). Writers who ignore or bypass the initial reaction, the prearticulated solution, produce response or analysis papers that are hollow, thin, unconvincing, and uninteresting.

To combat that tendency to jump to the cerebral, on the first day of a literature class I play a song that students don't know and that seems a poor candidate for a meaning hunt. I usually use "Fudge Bar" by Sinkhole, a spirited defense of the candy that is "the best by far," and an attack on the "lies" of those who say "Don't eat it." On the first listening, I ask students just to jot down a general impression—"amusing" or "lively" or "I hate this kind of thing." We listen a second time with instructions to pick out one element of the song that provokes the gut reaction, so "this kind of thing" becomes "singers who scream," while "lively" centers on "speedy drumming."

When the song is over, I ask students to read what they've written, find a word or combination of words that is interesting (surprising, confusing, contradictory; something they'd like to explore), and freewrite on it for five minutes. The student who hates screaming might freewrite on why she hates punk but loves Janis Joplin, who screamed in another era. The drumming fan might ponder whether he usually responds most strongly to energy in music.

Finally, after rereading their freewrites, students write a sentence—it could be called a thesis statement, but I usually avoid the term—that summarizes what they're thinking and connects the specific detail to the generalization. In the process, they make sense of their reactions, moving from the visceral to the more intellectual or analytic. Why did they react as they did? What in their background, their history with this genre, perhaps their struggles with dieting contributed to the initial laugh or "yuck"? In the discussion that follows, we might find that Rachel doesn't like punk because her sister's loser boyfriend plays it. Justin is a classical music fan who turns off at the first screamed word. Marie wants to get up and dance—it reminds her of the bands at her high school dances.

Such associations may seem tangential and distracting, but they often provide the best starting place for an exploration that will lead to a valuable critical insight. As Jon D. Green writes, quoting Suzanne Langer,

> "Intuition is the basic process of all understanding" and is "just as operative in discursive thought as in clear sense perception and immediate judgment" [Langer, 29]. In other words, the gut reactions that prompt us occasionally to notice some striking similarity between two seemingly unrelated works of art are often reliable cues to deeper structural and functional similarities. (12)

Green makes explicit his "commitment to individual subjective responses as the foundation for any comparative analysis" and worries that we "have lost sight of the 'holistic view' [Gombrich, Hochberg, and Black, 48] afforded by the unifying intuitive efforts of the imagination and the emotions" (14).

Even if they wanted to, listeners/readers couldn't eliminate their nonintellectual, nonanalytical responses, whether we call them intuition, gut feeling, or felt sense. So I encourage students to accept their initial reactions, wherever they come from, and build an analysis that incorporates them, rather than try to drive them from their minds.

Rachel writes a miniature argument about how punk lyrics and punk culture encourage punk listeners to be losers. Justin defines "singing" in a way that excludes the "Fudge Bar" vocal. Marie writes about how punk has been popular for twenty-five years because people with energy like dancing to the insistent, frenetic drum beat. Even if none of the students develops these ideas any further, they've had a good demonstration of how gut feeling—some preanalytical, usually unarticulated sense—can (and, I would argue, usually does) provide the basis and the material for productive analysis.

I emphatically do not see this movement from personal reaction to more analytical discussion as being useful only for personal essays or creative nonfiction. Students cannot afford to ignore their personal associations with their writing subject, even if that subject is economics or marine biology. When confronted with a research paper assignment about tidal pools, a marine biology student might begin with her interest in seaweed and her memory of how different seaweeds tasted when she was a kid. The economics student who recently developed an interest in political science might write a paper about the political value of perpetuating the myth of a "free market."

To provide an example of the sometimes Byzantine path from reaction to analysis, I usually describe my thought process the first time I played "Fudge Bar" for class. I liked the music, but I thought that the words were kind of silly for punk. My history with punk prepared me for anger or angst, big thoughts about freedom, sexuality, moral responsibility, rage against "bottled violence" (Minor Threat) or the Queen (Sex Pistols) or self (Nirvana). But a fudge bar?

Focusing on the specific lyric that hooked me—the repeated "lies!"—led me to a more satisfying intellectual understanding of the gut reaction. The song in fact does fulfill my desire for punk to be revolutionary. On the issue of unhealthy foods—sugar and fat—the cultural voices of health and reason unite in their condemnation. So championing something full of "chocolate butter" is a blow against an empire, a questioning of authority as surely as is the more common finger flung in the fogy's face. This train of thought could lead to a paper about the sense of rebellion necessary to punk and the various ways that different groups rebel.

The very ordinary subject and the extraordinary treatment of it catch students' attention. Two years after I played "Fudge Bar" in class, Aaron wrote me that he still remembered "Fudge bar you are the best by far," still recalled some of the teaching lessons associated with the song (Croft).

Only thirty minutes have elapsed, yet we've gone from gut to head, integrating both, seeing how an apparently idiosyncratic, unhelpful, unthesislike initial reaction in fact reveals something about the song, the genre, and the listener. We've demonstrated that inarticulate, seemingly irrational and perhaps even irrelevant reactions—things that many teachers would call wrong—can be articulated, their logic revealed, their legitimacy supported. Students may well decide that their initial reaction was too idiosyncratic, too casual, too silly to be worth developing into any kind of analysis, but they should at least conclude that the reaction wasn't stupid. There was some kind of logic behind it, a rational train of associations. They can pursue that train further if they like, or mentally set that initial reaction aside and work on other reactions, other elements. But with some understanding of why they reacted as they did, and some validation of their reactions, they're less likely to feel that their ideas are wrong, evidence of their shortcomings as critical readers.

Throughout the semester, I remind students of this process of interweaving thought and feeling and encourage them to experiment with new iterations of it. (See the end of this chapter for one such iteration.) This may be a first step for students toward trusting their own reactions and feelings. Many have concluded that their feelings are always wrong, since their teachers often seem to reject students' opinions and find things in the text that students don't see at all. So I am at pains to help students see the legitimate value behind divergent reactions, to stop thinking in terms of right and wrong and try to mine every reaction for some nugget.

Of course, once you open the discussion to any associations in student minds, strange possibilities may arise. A student from Brooklyn said he couldn't think positively about "Fudge Bar" because, in the slang he grew up with, "fudge bar" meant a turd and "chocolate butter" was diarrhea. With those images in mind, he couldn't pay attention to my political reading of the song, but of course his reaction taught a perfect lesson in how radically what readers bring to a text can affect their readings.

Seeing with Different Eyes

Christenson and Roberts report on a particularly interesting study that provides convincing evidence for how strongly listeners' and viewers' social context determines what they see and hear. The researchers showed a Madonna music video, "Papa Don't Preach," to college students and then asked them a number of questions about it, including What do you think this video is about? In the video, "a young woman falls for a young man, becomes pregnant, then struggles with how to tell her father that she intends to keep the baby" (167). In their reactions, almost all (97 percent) of the white women mentioned pregnancy, while fewer than half (43 percent) of the black men did. In contrast, both black men and women mentioned the father/daughter relationship twice as often as their white counterparts. The researchers suggest that differences in cultural attitudes toward unwed pregnancy might account for these disparate reactions: "Black girls who become pregnant out of wedlock can expect more favorable reactions from the baby's father, their families, and their peers than can White girls in the same situation" (167). Whether or not the researchers have put their finger on the key issue, clearly some difference in the backgrounds of the white and black students led them to emphasize very different elements in the same video.

This study raises issues for teachers beyond the simple caution against ranking one particular interpretation over another. We must confront questions about what we mean by "reading comprehension" and whether testing such comprehension is as straightforward an assessment of "reading skills" as the testers would like us to believe. I imagine if I had seen the video, I would have said, "Of course it's about pregnancy." But I'm beginning to see those "of course" moments as the most dangerous ones, times when we need to make the most effort to shake ourselves loose from our own assumptions and try to understand other interpretations.

The Value of Misreading

While we need to be careful about ruling out or choosing only certain interpretations, sometimes particular interpretations seem indisputably "wrong" because they're derived from something as basic as misunderstanding words. Yet even these misreadings have value.

Green Day's "Brat" blasts as loud as I dare crank it at the beginning of the third day of class. The students are awake, some grinning with recognition, some puzzled about why this balding English prof is playing annoying pop-punk. I've got their attention. Now I want to change their minds about mistakes.

Janet Emig and others woke us to the value of developmental errors; Mina Shaughnessy prompted us to search more systematically and sympathetically into the reasons for writing mistakes; Don Murray (1983) and Bruce Ballenger (1990) even encourage us to invite error, cultivate it, search it for the creative spark, the unexpected connection, the striking metaphor.

But students who have been punished with red marks for years and who struggle to prevent their reappearance do not easily swallow this liberal thinking about mistakes. They've never been inspired by the admonitions *tense!* or *awk* scrawled in their margins. Using the wrong word embarrasses them, like appearing in public with a zit still bleeding, a blunder you want to fix as quickly as possible and then drive from your mind.

They're less likely to be so uptight about mistakes in their grasp of pop culture. They have all misheard and misimitated song lyrics without great trauma. Part of the fun of rock music—and of television commercials and music videos—is gradually figuring out opaque lyrics, and you don't want to wait until you get them all before you start singing the song. No doubt in junior high some kids tease others about their inaccurate rendition of Top-40 choruses, but soon such nastiness often turns to cooperation, as Beatles fans in the sixties shared clues to try to determine if Paul really was dead.

When I first bought Green Day's album, I tell my class, I liked "Brat," but of course I didn't look at the lyrics right away, or even the title. I just liked the opening, where in a typically whiny, aggressive tone, singer Billie Joe announces that his parents aren't looking so odd anymore. I didn't follow the story line, but I liked the idea of this snotty teenager realizing that he had more in common with his parents than he had thought. Maybe he had had a revelation about how rapidly he was growing to resemble them. I began singing the line around the house, and soon my son, six, began to sing it too, a gesture that would warm the heart of any parent, especially one almost four decades older than his son.

Finally, after singing the line a few dozen times, I began to ask myself what the song was about, and I looked at the lyrics. Turns out the Brat is not exactly a heartwarming neoBeaver. He's just waiting for his parents to die so he can live off their money. He doesn't say they're looking less *odd*; he says they're looking less *hot*. It is an upbeat opener, from the Brat's perspective—the worse his parents look, the sooner he may get his inheritance.

My substitution of *odd* for *hot* led me to create an interpretation that says almost nothing about the song itself, and I could just have dismissed my reading with some comment about wax in the ears. But my interpretation does say a lot about me, my desire not to seem too alien to my kids, my worries about being over the hill and out of it. It's not much of a start for a critical analysis, but possibly a valuable entry into a personal essay, a personal analysis.

And it's the kind of insight from error that I hope my students cultivate, instead of worrying about perfection or author's intention. The song allows me to *show* the value of productive mistakes. As does the exercise with "Fudge Bar," this quick musical expedition encourages students to look for inspiration and meaning not just in the texts they study but in their emotional reactions to those texts, their assumptions, their interpretations, whether or not they're faithful to the text. As any English teacher knows, analysis papers very often say more about the student writer than about the text, even when the author intends to focus solely on the text. Looking at mistakes as a vein to mine rather than a source of embarrassment can bring out into the open the relationship between text and reader and help students develop new and more sophisticated attitudes toward it. As Michael Jarrett puts it, "there's every reason to cultivate strategies of misreading: They lead to creativity" (198). Anthony DeCurtis writes about Jerry Garcia, "There could be no such thing as a mistake; every direction pulsed with potential revelation" (95).

Perhaps we should abandon the term *misreading* altogether, since it seems to imply that a "right" reading exists, somewhere beyond our grasp. As Rosenblatt and others have argued, meaning is a construction in time created by a recursive transaction of reader and text, so all reading is misreading, as each reader adds pieces to the text or ignores elements in the text. In fact, as the editors of *Relocating Cultural Studies* point out, some texts (they focus on Michael Jackson's *Thriller* album) may be popular precisely because they allow so many readings, because they provide "a complex cultural medium in which 40,000,000 consumers could successfully invest meanings" (Blundell, Shepherd, and Taylor, 8).

Demanding Ambiguity

One reaction to a world that can be read so many ways is to insist on a narrowing of choices. As William Perry showed more than thirty years ago, many students come to college as simple dualists, absolutists, black-or-white thinkers, believers in right, wrong, and authority. They view ambiguity with suspicion and condescension—if you weren't so lame, they seem to think, you'd be one thing or another. They may have been encouraged to hunt for clues to figure out whether the answer is A or B. "It could be both" is seen as a failure of detective work, an insult to the intellect.

Ambiguity *is* sometimes the result of misreading; Green Day's portrait of the Brat is thoroughly negative, once you hear the words as they were written. (Singers who sing unintelligibly and don't provide lyric sheets obviously increase the possibilities of ambiguity.) But to become sophisticated readers who can see beyond right and wrong to the layers and complexities of most texts, students need to be prepared for ambiguity within the text itself, for the possibility that the text includes both A and B, despite their apparent incompatibility. We don't have to mention the word *deconstruction* to introduce students to its insights.

Lou Reed's "Heroin" provides a useful example of ambiguity as it shows several sides of a subject that we train kids to think of as straightforward and one-sided: illegal drugs (Velvet). The song takes one of the country's most feared drugs and complicates it, explaining addiction realistically, acknowledging that for so many smart people to get hooked, it must include genuine pleasure and can't be all the painful screams of withdrawal in John Lennon's "Cold Turkey." The narrator is ecstatic about the initial rush of heroin but admits it will someday kill him. Contradictory evidence piles up, the dream and nightmare mix, while the cello plays a single protracted note, the drone of addiction in the back of the addict's life, which at the end finally breaks into a screaming frenzy.

Evaluating Different Interpretations

While Lou Reed may leave us confused about whether ambiguities can ever be unraveled, getting students to "hear" the lyrics of a Dylan song can establish that for many listeners, one version, one interpretation of the lyrics is more convincing, more "right." And as we discuss the merits of different interpretations, we also learn some important lessons about revision.

Before I plug in my boom box, I hand out the lyrics to "I Want You" (www.bobdylan.com/songs/wantyou.html). Both a hit single and the catchiest tune on Dylan's epic 1966 album, *Blonde on Blonde*, the song has always been one of my favorites, with its bouncy beat and cheerful guitar. Yet when people who have never heard the song read the lyrics, they imagine a slow, tormented, yearning wail. The singer complains about everything from the "guilty undertaker" to "silver saxophones" that conspire against the singer and against the singer's relationship to the song's "you"; only the singer's bravado insistence that "I wasn't born to lose you" offers any hope for the relationship.

After students have read the lyrics, I ask them about the tone of the words and the music that should accompany them: happy or sad? fast or slow? pained or proud? We explore for a minute where their expectations come from; most point to evidence of the singer's pain and difficulties and expect and predict a slow, tormented song, perhaps somewhat like the Beatles' or Elvis Costello's versions of "I Want You."

Students often look puzzled when they first hear the music; some laugh with embarrassment, thinking I sure blew that. It's a happy song after all. I play them a verse and a chorus, ask if it sounds the way they expected it to ("No! It's so upbeat and cheerful"), then say a word or two about revision as I cue Dylan's 1979 *Live at Budokan* album.

I haven't a clue how Dylan goes about revising his songs, but it seems at least possible that he rethought the music for "I Want You" as a result of listening to the words of his own text. Maybe he heard the pain and longing that most students read in the lyrics and decided that the happy bounce of the original tune undermined that longing. Whether or not he went through such a process, by imaginatively constructing it, the class can gain insight into the maxim, Let your text be your guide. Listening to your text, following its directions, noting its promises and gaps is, I think, the best solution to a lot of student revision worries—How do I know what to change? Should I listen to my peers' suggestions? How do I know I'm not making things worse? We have to become experts at listening to our own texts, hearing the voice and the tone and the focus in the words we've written, and revealing, supporting, building on those things as we revise. Of course, we must always leave open the possibility that the direction or tone or emphasis of the existing text should change, that, in Dylan's case, the words should be made happier to reflect the tone of the music. But such a decision—which leads to the kind of major revision that I applaud—can be made only when the writer has listened carefully to tone and tried to see the text as others might.

I can't judge whether the revised version of "I Want You" is better (personally, I think they're both terrific), but it certainly emphasizes the pained longing many people read in the lyrics. It satisfies students that they weren't in fact "wrong" in their perception of the lyric voice. It may convince them that revision isn't for losers and amateurs—Dylan had no reason to mess with a very successful song, yet mess with it he did. Maybe there's more to a subject they considered finished. And it may leave them with new questions and outlooks about ambiguity: Is it all right for different elements of a piece to be working at cross-purposes? How does it affect their understanding of interpretation and meaning when the artist himself creates much of the ambiguity?

James W. Penha provides another example of how we intuitively connect certain kinds of music with certain lyrics. He has his classes write to Tchaikovsky's Piano Concerto no. 1 as an experiment in prosody, in hearing the music of words.

> Some student always asks, "Why do writers bother with rhythm at all?" I draw attention to the fact that most members of the class, having heard the romance in Tchaikovsky's concerto, invariably write lyrics to love songs. (79)

Interpretation and Creation

When does an interpretation shade into a creation? *Creative* and *original* are loaded words, and for many people, "creative" writing includes only fiction, poetry, and drama, off in a corner of the writing world by themselves. To help students see that their expository or analytical writing is not just busy work for drones, we need to break down the false dichotomy between *creation* and *interpretation,* to demonstrate that building on someone else's ideas, text, or melody can be tremendously creative (cf. Shakespeare), while venturing into the purely created worlds of fantasy can produce writing that is familiar and stale.

Do we call John Coltrane's version of the traditional song "Greensleeves" a creation or an interpretation? In only a small percentage of the tune is the original melody recognizable. While Traditional gets songwriting credits, Coltrane—and pianist McCoy Tyner and a dozen other musicians—contribute way more than whatever British troubadour first sang the song. But can we be sure that he contributed more to the final product than does the singer who sings "Ode to Joy" exactly as it's written, or the actor who recites every word of *Hamlet?* I see more originality in Coltrane's music than in these other productions, but I bet I would get arguments from classical musicians and actors. In any case, discussing such issues in class can complicate students' understanding of what is *creative* versus *original* and perhaps can help them see more value and room for their own thinking in the kinds of writing they do in school.

Artistic Conversations

Assessing the validity, value, and originality of an interpretation often involves considering that interpretation in light of ongoing conversations about the subject matter. Writers in every field talk to each other through their creations; they're part of a "discourse community," if we must, a group bonded by language, interests, and perspectives. As I pointed out in the introduction, many current theorists and teachers feel it's important to make students aware of the existence of such communities and become conversant in the ways different communities communicate. At least theoretically, such conversations should empower students; learning how to talk and act like a good student may bring students more success than learning the subject better.

In other parts of this book, I discuss artistic conversations between Van Morrison and Patti Smith (Chapter 1) and between X and the Doors (Chapter 6). Speech of Arrested Development also began his career conversing with one of his musical forebears, Sly Stone of Sly and the Family Stone. Arrested Development's "People Everyday" reverses the title of Sly's hit, "Everyday People," while copying the chorus with subtle alterations to make funk rock into hip-hop. Demonstrating that the process of reshaping past and present is ongoing, Arrested Development added at the end of the disc another version of the song, a "Metamorphosis Mix" not identified on the CD insert or cover. Everyday people keep growing.

In the realm of classical music, Barrett, McCoy, and Veblen discuss at length a conversation between contemporary composer Ellen Taaffe Zwilich and George Frederick Handel; Zwilich's "Concerto Grosso

1985" quotes and borrows its title from Handel. Students might be interested in imagining a more recent fantasy conversation between the Ramones, one of the first American punk bands, all of whom adopted the same last name, and the Donnas, a current California speedy punk band whose members are all named Donna. What have the Donnas borrowed from the Ramones? What have they added that's uniquely theirs? Does it affect our appreciation of them to view their music as derivative? Were the Ramones derivative as well?

If I had any hip-hop fans in my class, I would ask them for suggestions about a current conversation I could play, because the technique of sampling—borrowing segments of recorded sounds and integrating them into new creations—has radically increased the number and the kind of musical conversations. Initially popularized by rap artists, sampling is used throughout the musical world now. Listen to a few minutes of your students' favorites and you'll probably hear echoes of your era, whatever that era might be. Some songs use samples or cover versions in homage to the original, others to mock the original. Some develop clear, obvious conversations, like that between the Beastie Boys' "Fight for Your Right (to Party)" and Public Enemy's "Party for Your Right to Fight." Students who like the Fugees' 1996 version of "Killing Me Softly" might want to imagine a conversation with Roberta Flack, who had a big hit with the song in 1973. At first the Fugees' Lauryn Hill seems almost to be mocking Flack's gentle, classy, dignified version as she twists the words of the first chorus into "killing a soundboy with this sound" and interrupts the song with howls and static. But the next time around she sings the chorus more reverently, with harmonies that sound as though they were recorded in a church, and I'm left impressed with the beauty of Hill's voice and of the melody, wondering what students could tell me about the intentional clutter the Fugees added to the song. Such conversations broaden the meaning of the word *interpretation* and again complicate the distinction between interpretation and creation. They open the possibility that a work can be original—that is, substantially new—and yet require knowledge of another work to be fully meaningful.

Whenever we examine such a conversation, we ask, is there a meaning or a purpose to this conversation, and most important, how could we enter into it? Could we study the conversation and then add our own interpretation or creation? To take one example, there is value in thinking of the Fugees' "The Mask" and Paul Laurence Dunbar's "We Wear the Mask" as a "conversation" because the two say much more together than they do separately, and the question, What do they have to say to each other? is so intriguing (see Figure 4–1). Dunbar's poem presents the duplicity necessary to African American survival as a simple fact: "We wear the mask." No qualifications, no *sometimes*, no *if we feel like it.* At the brink of the century that many feel was dominated in America by the race question, Dunbar's narrator cries from behind the mask, demanding that the reader never again view the happy black cooks and mammies and porters with paternalistic satisfaction but at least wonder, Are they wearing the mask?

That a century later an important black hip-hop group would rap about the mask might seem to indicate that nothing has changed. But in the Fugees' song, the mask is an option, not a requirement. The song opens with a question. Do we still wear masks? For a moment, we can revel in the fantasy of a time when the answer will be *no.* Soon, however, we learn that everybody hides his or her identity with masks. But does *everybody* include whites as well as blacks, making the mask part of the human condition, rather than a demeaning but necessary concession that blacks must make to racist America? If so, then it would be possible to trace an evolution from Dunbar's time, when the mask hid the tormented souls of white America's Other, to Ralph Ellison's invisible narrator, who speaks for everyone, though no one else can see him, to the troubled (presumably black) characters in the Fugees' song, who apparently *are* everyone.

All of these conversations raise questions more often than they provide answers, but I agree with McNamee that "the expertise of the educator becomes his or her ability to 'keep the conversation going.'" We must as often as possible engage students in this conversation, asking for instance which account of the mask seems more effective, when and why they wear a mask, asking them to draw a mask or sing about a mask or find a picture of one on the Internet. Students generally haven't read enough or listened enough to make many connections between literary texts, but they can add their own perspective without knowing what the rest of the world has said. Having participated in such a conversation, students might be open to discussing the conversations that go on in their own disciplines.

Write: Gut Response to Literature

This chapter began with a multistep writing process that helps students develop what could be the beginning of an analytical paper from an initial gut reaction to a song. In a literature class, I always follow that initial musical exercise with a very similar work session for the first paper. When we're just beginning to talk about the first major assignment, I ask students to come to class having chosen the story or poem that they want to write about. Then they treat that text as we treated the song "Fudge Bar" at the beginning of the chapter, brainstorming or freewriting for a few minutes on a number of prompts and questions.

- What was your initial gut reaction to the text or to some part of the text?
- Can you isolate one specific element that provoked that reaction?
- Describe that element in detail or freewrite about it.
- Now analyze your reaction—what in your background, in the situation, in the text itself led to that reaction?
- Try to build on the initial reaction to the text an argument or thesis about the text. For instance, someone whose first reaction to "We Wear the Mask" was "me too" might initially feel embarrassed about claiming victim status. As racist and oppressive as our society is today, none of us—particularly those of us born with privileges of race and class—can fully appreciate the kind of world Dunbar wrote about, where elementary school textbooks reported the inferiority of Africans as fact, and African Americans could be lynched for dropping the mask and showing the white world who they really were and how they really felt. But going through this process might lead a white, middle-class student to write a paper about how Dunbar elicits white sympathy and invites the very reaction the student was feeling guilty about. In order to highlight the frustration he feels, Dunbar exploits the tendency of white readers to identify with the black predicament described in the poem. Thesis: Dunbar uses race-neutral language and imagery to invite all readers to sympathize with a fundamentally racial predicament.

Figure 4–1

We Wear the Mask

Paul Laurence Dunbar (1896)

We wear the mask that grins and lies,
It hides our cheeks and shades our eyes,—
This debt we pay to human guile;
With torn and bleeding hearts we smile,
And mouth with myriad subtleties.

Why should the world be overwise,
In counting all our tears and sighs?
Nay, let them only see us, while
    We wear the mask.

We smile, but, O great Christ, our cries
To thee from tortured souls arise.
We sing, but oh the clay is vile
Beneath our feet, and long the mile;
But let the world dream otherwise,
    We wear the mask!

Five

Constructing Meaning

Teaching is a process of making meaning.

> Sheila McNamee,
> communications professor, 2000

When you're listening to an Ice-T album you can agree or disagree. But you should never think everything I'm thinking, because then only one of us is thinking.

> Ice-T, rapper, 1991

Many students have a simple view of meaning—it is something put into a text (or a piece of music) by the artist, almost like a package dropped into the mail: if nothing interferes, and if the receiver follows the appropriate steps, the package will get to its destination intact, and the receiver will open and enjoy the fruitcake in much the same condition as it was sent. Building on many of the insights of the previous chapter, this one explores ways that music can be used to complicate students' understanding of meaning making and help students see that making meaning is a complex process involving many factors and contributions from receiver as well as creator. Chapter 4 concentrates on ways teachers can help students understand and value their own contributions to the development of interpretations; this chapter focuses more on the ways artists themselves try to control the meanings of their creations and on the variety of information sources from which readers/listeners can draw to construct the meaning of a text or piece of music.

Creating a Romantic Past

Neil Young's "Cortez the Killer" is as overtly political as his more famous "Ohio"; the title comments directly on the past five centuries of white and Native American conflict, and it alone was probably enough to get the song banned in Spain (http://hyperrust.org/Lyrics/Zuma.html). But in the United States, the song, though not radio friendly, has tremendous cachet among Young fans in part because the lyrics create a world that fit the romantic notions of the mid-70s rock audience, the world of Edenic natives and genocidal Europeans. The longing built up by the melody and the guitar introduction evolve into a yearning for that perfect prelapsarian past—a time before the sins of slavery, genocide, and ecocide stained the consciousness of every sensate North American. Young takes the romantic reconstruction of the Aztecs to an extreme until, perhaps aware of the hyperbole, he drops the history lesson entirely in the last verse and sings about a singular "she" who still haunts the singer, somewhat the way, one assumes, he's haunted by the image of Cortez arriving to wreak havoc.

Students who have difficulty seeing how a fiction writer uses setting and description to control readers' reactions may have less trouble understanding how Young quickly wins our allegiance to the Aztec side. It's easy to demonstrate how altering the details of the created world can quickly alter the world itself. Reading descriptions of the sacrifices that Young romanticizes can make the Aztecs human again and perhaps start a conversation about why it serves Young's purposes to create an idealized world. And a discussion of how Neil Young created one vision of the Aztecs and how student contributions can alter or expand that vision can be an effective first step in helping students see the complexities of how meaning is constructed by artist and audience.

Young's rather heavy-handed manipulation of listener sympathy can lead to a much more subtle analysis of the way writers influence readers' views, particularly about political topics. To get students thinking about politics, I have them read two short articles from opposite ends of the political spectrum, then use the appendices from Donald Lazere's article "Teaching the Political Conflicts: A Rhetorical Schema" to analyze the political stances of the writers. With Lazere's help, students can situate the piece politically by using the author's name, the name of the publication, the specific issues the author raises, the language the author uses, and the allies and opponents that the author mentions. A class period spent in poring over the articles and unmasking their politics can help students read more knowledgeably and be less easily affected by manipulation like Young's.

Meaning Reinterpreted

Often, the clues writers provide don't lead readers as rapidly toward a conclusion as Neil Young's details do. Ambiguity, if not confusion, may be the rule more than the exception in lyrics and poetry, and most students enjoy figuring out obscure words or bringing in crucial bits of information to make meaning of a song. The sleuthing involved in figuring out, for instance, that the Grateful Dead song "New Speedway Boogie" is about the murder of a fan at a free Rolling Stones concert at Altamont Speedway in 1969 resembles detective work enough that the process seems familiar to us. We all know the kind of work Sherlock Holmes does, even if we can't beat him to a solution. By contrast, we're less familiar with the kind of thinking that leads to a change in perception of something familiar and seemingly well understood.

Helping students to see new, different, perhaps even radical or blasphemous meanings in something familiar is a major step in convincing them of the subjectivity of interpretation, the slipperiness of meaning, and the radical changes of meaning that can be brought about if certain elements of the text are emphasized.

Every American child knows "The Star Spangled Banner." Some even know that it was written during the War of 1812, and they may have envisioned what it would look like to be viewing the flag through the "red glare" of rockets and bombs. But it took Jimi Hendrix to reveal the meaning of the anthem to us: it is a song inspired by war, about war, incorporating values and sentiments perhaps appropriate only for wartime. Imitating war sounds with his guitar, Hendrix provokes questions like Do we really want to be represented by a symbol associated with rockets and bombs? Is that the only light the flag looks good in? Would we be better off with a national symbol associated with images of peace and cooperation? Students with a little historical knowledge might suggest times when blind allegiance to the flag and all of its military representations led to grievous mistakes—during the wars against the Native Americans, the Filipinos, or the Vietnamese, for instance.

Hendrix doesn't pervert the words—as generations of schoolchildren have done—nor does he bring in outside information or impose his own interpretation. Merely by creating, audibly, the soundtrack that Francis Scott Key envisioned for his song, Hendrix makes the familiar new.

Similarly, Michael Jarrett's discussion of the song "Dixie" makes it a perfect—though potentially explosive—subject for class scrutiny. The song is still popular, and students have probably heard of the controversy about removing the Confederate flag from Southern statehouses. Does

"Dixie" deserve the same fate? Some people are "offended by the antebellum stereotypes it asks them to celebrate" while others are "nostalgically drawn to the idyllic scene it calls them to conjure" (27). Jefferson Davis had it played at his inauguration, but so did Abraham Lincoln. And the story of the song is the story of so much American culture. According to the book *Way Up North in Dixie: A Black Family's Claim to the Confederate Anthem* (Sacks and Sacks), Ben and Lew Snowden, the children of freed slaves, taught the song to Daniel Emmett, "the founder of the first professional blackface minstrel troupe" (Jarrett, 26), but of course Emmett got the credit and the success from it. Students could read about the song's history in Jarrett or in Barrett, McCoy, and Veblen (150–54) and then discuss the meaning they get out of the song, where that meaning comes from, and why others might react so differently to it.

Constructing an Illusion

Normally we must examine texts closely to construct meaning in the ways I've described so far in this chapter. But it is possible to look at texts too closely and to make meaning where there is none.

The great conspiracy theory of the 1960s could provide students with an opportunity to learn about the extent to which meaning is created in and limited to the mind of the beholder. No, I'm not talking about political assassinations; I'm talking about the "Paul is dead" illusion. It seems a little silly in retrospect, especially since Paul McCartney has outlived his wife, two partners, and his copyrights. But every 1960s Beatles fan was at least somewhat affected by the rumors, the clues, the puzzles that seemed to indicate that Paul was dead. There were clues in the songs, on the album covers, and especially in the records when played backward. Imagine how enthusiastic second-generation Beatles fans would be to learn research methods in pursuit of the McCartney mystery. Besides listening to the songs and trying to play old vinyl backward, students could research fanzines, visit hundreds of websites, and interview their parents or grandparents about what they remember, what clues they figured out.

And of course the research necessarily leads to an elegant postmodern question: Why did so many people see something that wasn't there? Did someone—a publicist, perhaps?—actually create the puzzle, or was the whole craze just evidence that Beatles fans were following their heroes into LSD? The ambiguities of such a search should leave any student with a healthy respect for the power of the individual or group to fabricate meaning and draw conclusions that may be both elegant and clever but may not correspond to anything else.

Tapping in to Schemata

People captivated by the "Paul is dead" paranoia or the related "Elvis lives" sightings had to create a schema, a network of interrelated beliefs and information, in which each piece of new information would fit. Clever writers, aware that all readers come to a text with such mental schema, activate or tap into these schema using key words or images, provoking a wealth of responses with very few words.

I start John Coltrane's "India" as soon as I get to class, but instead of writing the title on the board, I write, "What country is this song named after?" Almost always, students who are there at the beginning, when Coltrane's soprano sax takes off after the introduction by the two basses, say "India." Obviously Coltrane found something that provokes the schema "India" in the audience's mind. My guess is that he tapped into American stereotypes of Indian snake charmers. Often when they appear on TV or in movies, though the charmers are actually playing some kind of indigenous (I assume) flute, the soundtrack plays soprano sax.

Writers can make more productive word choices if they consciously think about the associations that readers bring to particular words. It's much easier to call up and build on a schema than it is to change it. If using the phrase "snake charmer music" is the most efficient way for a writer to conjure up the sound of a soprano sax in the reader's mind, then a clever writer will use it.

Beyond the Lyrics

> Well since she put me down / There's been owls pukin' in my bed.
> (Barry, 78)

The ability of the instrumental "India" to call up a single consistent image in readers' minds is unusual; discussing meaning in music almost inevitably leads to focusing on lyrics. I'm well aware that many of the insights and connections I make about songs in this book concern the lyrics, and that in reality many listeners either ignore the lyrics altogether or make them up because they can't understand them, as a young Dave Barry did with the first line of the Beach Boys' "Help Me Rhonda." The reasons for concentrating on lyrics are obvious: you can write them down and treat them the way you'd treat any other text; you can ask the same questions and point to the same issues as you would when discussing literature, so they're comfortable for English teachers to work with; they're user-friendly for students and teachers—they don't need to be put into words.

But we have to face the fact that, as Christenson and Roberts put it, "what most of us probably think of as the story or the 'message' is often—perhaps usually—ignored during the music listening . . . process" (116). Indeed, in one study, "Over a third [of the kids surveyed] could provide no interpretation whatsoever" of their three favorite songs (Christenson and Roberts, 157). It's important to keep in mind, however, the difference between being able to make sense of or summarize the meaning of an entire song, and liking, remembering a single line, and perhaps investing it with meaning. Apparently, very few listeners grasp the meaning of Bruce Springsteen's "Born in the USA," a story of a Vietnam vet who's been kicked all his life and has no future, but many, from Ronald Reagan to some music critics who should know better, have fixed on the apparently proud and certainly defiant chorus and assumed the song was optimistic and patriotic (Christenson and Roberts, 158–159, 164).

One alternative to the lyrical fixation is focusing on the arrangement and production of the song, the instrumentation and the studio innovations and insider information about the making of the record. But does it matter to the average listener how many tracks went into the making of a particular song or what technical innovations the engineer used?

Talking about nonverbal qualities of music is difficult, but sometimes it can reveal essential lessons about songs and other forms of writing. As John Lennon said, "You don't have to hear what Bob Dylan's saying, you just have to hear the way he says it" (Obstfeld and Fitzgerald, 222). Even just applying simple terms like *rough* or *smooth* or *happy* or *sad* can lead to important insights. In Chapter 4, I discuss how Dylan created two different musical atmospheres for his song "I Want You," one consonant with the way most people read the lyrics, the other a bouncy tune bucking the desperation of the lyrics. To get the point of the exercise, students have to describe both the music that they imagine and the music that they hear, but the simplest terms and the most vague reaction will do. If students describe the lyrics as sad and the tune as happy, the song can provide a model of apparent contradiction or deconstruction. And the realization that songs can succeed with seemingly warring musical elements can lead students to look for patterns of similar successes.

One of the fascinating effects in rock is the smooth, creamy voice—Morrissey's, say—riding on top of—against?—the rougher, driving guitar of someone like Johnny Marr (the guitarist in the Smiths when Morrissey was lead singer). Sleater-Kinney has taken such mixtures a step further, using an angry, shrill voice, a calmer, mellower voice, *and* two guitars. That such mixtures can succeed may prepare students to accept and appreciate other artistic mixtures—black humor, for instance, which mixes the comic with the horrible or morbid, or the many forms of irony. It may be that students who appreciate the Smiths' mixed smooth/harsh sound have a head start on enjoying Flannery O'Connor, who can make us laugh about a woman losing her wooden leg. And articulating the mixed effects of "I Want You" or Sleater-Kinney's "Burn, Don't Freeze" may help introduce students to deconstruction.

When listeners and readers are trying to think beyond the meaning of words to the other aspects of the song, the inability to understand lyrics can be an advantage. Some bands have a consistent musical tone not dependent on lyrics, and having students determine how that tone is created can help them analyze the music itself. The band Morphine, for instance, produced music that is as consistently dark as any I know. Not the exaggerated dark of Marilyn Manson's shock rock, but the kind of dark that, in retrospect, makes sense for a guy—band leader Mark Sandman—who named his band after a narcotic, called one of his albums *Cure for Pain*, and died on stage at age thirty-seven. Critics called it "noir rock," "modern-crime jazz," "the thinking man's uptown funk," "low rock" (Wener). But where does that darkness come from? Is it the unusual instrumentation—a unique two-string slide bass guitar, a baritone sax, and drums? Does having much of the musical interest center on the low end of the musical scale produce a feeling of heaviness and doom? Is it Sandman's voice? Is it the melodies or the particular way the instruments are played?

I don't think a teacher would get too many complaints for assigning students to describe and analyze the musical tone of their favorite band. And such an exercise would drive home a crucial point—you need to come up with a good description *and* explain or justify it.

The Medium Is the Message

To take students beyond the meaning of the lyrics, Marshall McLuhan's famous insight, the heading of this section, is as important today as it was in the 1960s, and it applies especially well to my ubiquitous music maker, the boom box. My 'box is always functional, utilitarian, small and light enough that I can tote it around campus from my office to every classroom, not one of those huge things that you have to carry on your shoulder and that used to be called derogatorily a ghetto blaster.

In the 1970s, when boom boxes began to seep into the American consciousness, they were treated as an absurd product of the inner-city ghetto. Primarily the province of black teenagers, they were scorned by white society and viewed with racist condescension, and cartoons abounded in which the size and weight of the boom box overwhelmed its carrier. They were from the ghetto, and they blasted, so no white kid would be caught dead with one.

Then, seemingly overnight, every college dorm room in America acquired at least one, and they became almost as commonplace as telephones. The message contained in this medium, then, is the same message we gain by looking at the history of African American music and language and fashion and sports and attitude: white culture denigrates anything identifiably black, says it doesn't fit within the bounds of decency, calls it primitive and uncivilized, spews upon it storms of invective—even while the more adventurous members of the influential white culture are already appropriating it, imitating black jive or black jazz or black basketball moves. These days it takes just weeks for America's scorn to turn into infatuation, not the months or years it took for whites to accept and imitate Dixieland or the blues or the Twist or fancy dunks. But our memories are so short, it seldom seems to dawn on whites that they're copying black innovations. As Riesman puts it, "the majority is continuously engaged in the process of adapting elements of the minority's musical outlook, while overtly ignoring or denigrating minority patterns" (9). And, the editors of *Relocating Cultural Studies* say, the capitalist system "has been increasingly successful in co-opting, recycling, and remarketing previous forms of oppositional expression" (Blundell, Shepherd, and Taylor, 8). It's a process we need to pay attention to.

So the boom box can both reinforce McLuhan's point about the medium and highlight an important lesson about cultural dynamics, the borrowing that keeps the dominant culture vibrant and fresh, though it seldom rewards or acknowledges its debt to the minority culture. The lesson of the boom box has stuck with me. It explains how rap can be so reviled by a white culture that buys millions of rap records and swoons for white rappers like Vanilla Ice, the Beastie Boys, and Eminem. Tony Van Der Meer says, "There is something horribly wrong with a dominant community repeatedly co-opting the cultural forms of oppressed communities, stripping them of vitality and form—the heritage of their creators—and then popularizing them" (5).

As Michael Jarrett points out in a particularly clever section of *Sound Tracks*, such insights into the tendency of commercial culture to profit from pale imitations of the products of innovators, often black, can lead to a "romantic, and, ultimately, racist" view of music, with authentic African Americans creating the real thing and white musicians and producers cleaning it up and bleaching it for a white audience.

Jarrett doesn't deny that this paradigm has some validity, but he suggests "an alternative way of viewing the history of popular music and the process of conventionalization," a view borrowed from, of all things, mushrooms (193). Fungi live on dead organic matter, breaking it down so that it can be reused. "Rock 'n' roll . . . feeds off the decay of tradition. It treats culture as compost. . . . Conventionalization is the compost from which innovation grows. It fosters artistic renewal by generating conditions that allow for aberrant readings or interpretations" (195). Therefore, innovation requires convention.

Though this insight may seem to be merely a bit of linguistic and metaphorical sleight of hand, I believe it can lead to a fundamental shift in the way those of us who are interested in innovation treat convention, in literature as well as in music. The fungal metaphor could be appropriated by any literature teacher trying to inspire students who appreciate one era or school of writing to see that their favorites, rather than abandoning or overthrowing the previous school, simply grew new fruit from its compost.

Other issues about music "media" are worth raising; almost inevitably, they have parallels in the world of literature and in the larger culture. Students who have grown up with only one recording medium—the CD—may need to do some research (the kind they would likely enjoy) to appreciate how much the recording medium influences the way listeners hear their music and in fact what music they listen to at all. In his study of British "motorbike boys" of the 1970s, Paul Willis notes the boys' preference for 78 rpm records over 45s, and for 45s over 33 rpm albums. With single-play records (most 45s and 78s, but not 33s), the listener selects each song individually and, if the listener's taste is for fast music with a big beat (the motorbike boys' preference), the listener can ensure that he listens to nothing but that genre. When playing a "long playing" album, however, the listener is forced either to treat it as a 45, moving the needle after each song, or endure someone else's song selection and order, putting up with slow songs.

Albums, as Willis indicates, appealed to the sedentary, "the expert or the devotee or the technician" (49). Tapes are the preferred musical medium only of people who listen to music mostly in cars or on boom boxes. CDs can potentially satisfy both the singles listener, who chooses to listen only to particular cuts, and the album listener, who treats the disc as a long record that doesn't need to be flipped over. But is that the reason for their sudden popularity? Some suggest that the takeover of CDs had more to do with strong-arm tactics by the music industry trying to deal with flat cassette and record sales (Negativland). Students may be conscious enough of their own listening practices to be able to investigate how the medium—and their ability to manipulate the medium—affects what they listen to and how they listen. If so, I would ask them one question for starters— Does the ability to pick and choose cuts on a CD mean that they never listen to cuts on favorite CDs that don't immediately strike their fancy? With LPs, changing records or skipping tracks was such a pain that most people would play a whole side at once, and after a number of listenings, the initially uninteresting song might become a favorite. My guess is that such gradual interest developed after repeated listening occurs less often with CDs.

A brief focus on these media issues in music can provide the basis for discussing similar issues about the written world. Do students prefer short stories to novels? Do they like novels like *Generation X* (Coupland) or *The Things They Carried* (O'Brien) written in chunks that may appeal to short attention spans? How is reading on the screen different from reading in a magazine or a book? How does the ascendancy of e-mail affect our communication and work habits? Are letters obsolete? What messages do we gather from the medium of e-mail, and how are they inherently different from the messages of the telephone or business letter? What new sources of meaning and confusion have sprung up with new media—the jargon of e-mailing, sensitivities to all caps, worries about viruses and worms? And yes, courageous teachers with lots of extra class time could open the big can of worms and ask for comments about the "message" of music videos.

Making the Windowpane Visible

"Good writing is like a windowpane," George Orwell declared; we don't want to see the pane, we want to see through it to whatever's outside. But Bruce Pirie, in *Reshaping High School English,* castigates English teachers for allowing the windowpane to stay invisible for their students, permitting them to treat fictional characters as real people, without giving any thought to why and how they were made as they were. Students need to learn, he says, that "a 'text' is not a simple pipeline to reality, but a constructed representation of reality" (22). He praises one class of students who were "explicitly aware that the artifacts they were examining—samples of television dramas— were constructions," their final form influenced by personal, social, political, and economic factors (19). This desire to understand the effects of the particular way a piece of art is created or presented is not new: Fifty years ago, David Riesman asked, "Can it be established that this mode of presentation [music "atomized into individual 'hits'"] reinforces the disconnectedness often associated with modern urban life?" (9). Such questions are as relevant as ever, and as music—especially in its commercially debased forms—infuses every cultural space from the dentist's office to the airplane seat, issues about the music business—and the publishing business—continue to multiply. We need to keep asking ourselves, Why was this piece included in this anthology? and Why is this the third new edition in five years? Similarly, it's valuable to analyze and speculate about why certain music reaches our ears, why some things make it big. As Johnny Temple writes, the tastes of young Americans "have long been dictated by trends set in the offices of music conglomerates [because] the major record companies have succeeded in erecting a pay-to-play industry that effectively shuts out any band whose label cannot pony up hundreds of thousands of dollars for radio, video, retail, and print promotion" (17). That's why expanding, analyzing, and challenging those tastes is in itself a political act.

As I was working on this chapter, the National Academy of Recording Arts and Sciences got some free press by awarding three Grammys to Eminem, the white rapper whose ostensibly misogynistic and homophobic lyrics provoked outrage. Defending the awards, critics pointed to the rapper's sophisticated use of frames and masks and applauded his blunt engagement of issues of race and sexuality. Many supporters of the awards sought to distance themselves from the lyrics but argued that they had no right to shut up or punish Eminem, no matter how distasteful his lyrics. But their defense made it sound as though the Grammys were a hunt for street talent, the decision made by walking from band to band, listening to the various musicians, choosing them on their merits. In other words, the *business* of music was made to seem invisible. But of course no Grammy committee or audience gets to choose from all the music being made in the country that year. Before Eminem could win an award, he had to persuade scores, perhaps hundreds, of people in the music business to support him—agents, bankers, engineers, producers, record company executives all up and down the line, and radio DJs. At any point, someone could have said "No, I don't like this" and the rest of the world might never have heard of Eminem.

Perhaps every one of those people held his or her nose and gave Eminem a stamp of approval, saying "Personally, I find it repugnant, but the music is so terrific (or "the First Amendment is so powerful") that I can't turn it down." But if Eminem's message were truly repugnant to all those businesspeople, he would not have made it. The crowning of Eminem reflects widely held American values as much as does the success of McDonald's or Wal-Mart. As Richard Kim writes in *The Nation*, "a really good dialogue on homophobia, violence, and entertainment . . . might start by seeing Eminem not as an exception but as the rule—one upheld not just by commercial entertainment values but by our courts, schools, family structures and arrangements of public space" (5).

On the day I talked about Eminem in class, I didn't want to promote him by playing his music, so instead I played a band in many ways Eminem's opposite. Veteran music critic Robert Christgau has called Sleater-Kinney "the world's greatest rock band" (quoted in Cvetkovich and Phillips, 16). They write songs in an array of styles and tones, their subject matter—including lesbian relationships—is often controversial, and some of their songs (e.g., "Not What You Want") rock as hard as anything I know. Everything about them challenges the music establishment, and what success they have achieved has been on their own terms, on the Kill Rock Stars label. I haven't heard anyone publicly decry their message. No one has to. Perhaps they choose to remain relatively obscure, to retain control of their music and avoid selling out. Many singer-songwriters who would be potential superstars on big labels—Greg Brown and Ani DiFranco come to mind—stick with their independent labels precisely because they value such integrity and creative control, and some discerning music listeners seek out "indie" labels to hear genuine music.

Either way—whether by conscious choice or by industry rejection—Sleater-Kinney's progressive message and music won't, in the present state of the music industry, reach the same number of ears as Eminem's vitriol. While I have the utmost respect for this approach to musical success, it keeps Sleater-Kinney out of the spotlight. In 2001, all twenty-one of my students had heard of Eminem, only one of Sleater-Kinney.

There are no doubt countless other aspects of the music business that students would enjoy and understand analyzing; but it might take some imagination to tie some of these aspects to English. For instance, a teacher who wanted to discuss the publishing business and the effects of the increasingly concentrated, profit-oriented publishing houses on what we read might start by looking at the same issue in music. For instance, baby boomers with a closet full of old Beatles LPs might contrast the way Capitol, the Beatles' American record company, released their music with the way Parlophone originally brought the Beatles to the British. The American albums are shorter and more numerous, sometimes padded with filler, leading inevitably to the conclusion that

Capitol was trying to wring more albums—and therefore more profit—out of the Beatles' output, musical coherence and integrity be damned.

Literary scholars have long discussed similar ways that market forces have influenced what we read. Teachers can draw parallels from any era of the literary world with which they're conversant. We can see in the *Iliad* and the *Odyssey* evidence of how "publication" medium—oral recitation—affects the text: rhyme, rhythm, and repeated phrases made the recitation easier. In *The Rise of the Novel,* Ian Watt argues that the British novel arose in the eighteenth century in response to the growth of a largely female middle class with time and income to spend on reading. Lovers of nineteenth-century novels can point to the effects of serial publication or of authors' being paid by the word. Even most eight-year-olds know how publishers' desires to sell the next issue dictate that every comic end in the middle of a tantalizing plot line. And students who read best-seller lists or hang out in paperback bookstores can attest to publishers' abilities to respond ever more quickly to the latest fad or news event. But we can only speculate about what books these instant sellers elbow aside.

Classes interested in how business priorities have affected literature might also look at how the huge advances for books (and records) to celebrities has affected the publishing world. Publishing ownership, distribution, and resources have become concentrated in a few huge companies, and they like to wager on a few blockbuster books. What long-term effects does such an emphasis have on American reading habits? What happened to the days when publishers kept a long list in print, including hundreds of marginally profitable titles? Is it possible to imagine, from our capitalist-triumphant point of view, that some publishers used to see their job as finding and publishing great books, regardless of their sales potential?

The Dangers of Musical Meaning-Making

While much of our attention is directed to understanding how and why a song or text takes on meanings, sometimes it's just as important to challenge and resist meanings. If I were teaching younger people, I think I would spend a good deal more time directly confronting the kind of simplified, catch-phrase thinking that some songs seem to encourage. I warn against such oversimplification in my discussion of "Down by the River" (see Chapter 1). Other examples are easy to find. What view of marriage does Kurt Cobain convey in "All Apologies" when he equates marriage and burial? How would you feel about that song if you were his widow?

While the media focus on young people who seem to take song lyrics as instructions for suicide or mayhem, a larger and more pervasive question is how a given text constructs its audience. Some supporters of Eminem and other musical acts that sing about violence, misogyny, and homophobia insist that rather than promote such antisocial behaviors, the music mocks them, asking us to question or laugh at them. As a longtime fan of the music of Frank Zappa, I can accept the notion that what some listeners hear as promotion of offensive behavior others hear as satire. But when viewed in terms of the audience that such music creates and the responses of that audience, is it better for an audience to chuckle than to cheer at an account of spouse abuse? I agree with Pirie that "For any text, we can ask students what kind of ideal audience is being constructed," whether they feel comfortable being part of that audience, and whether they can successfully resist becoming part of it (30).

The important songs to analyze in this connection are, of course, the ones in the student's own head, which is one reason why, at the beginning of every writing course, I encourage students to write down the title of a song in their heads or in their CD players and then analyze, at least briefly, why that particular song has taken up residence and what it says about them (see Chapter 1).

The ability of a song to crystallize a person's thinking about a particular issue is a fascinating subject that I've never seen adequately explored. Are we attracted to a song's simple formulation because it perfectly articulates something we've felt but have been unable to voice? Or is the process by which a song takes on personal meaning for us likely to be more insidious, the song boiling down the complex and multifaceted into the simplified and sometimes banal? Do songs have the power to change the original emotion, gradually taking over the individual's thinking, so that the listener eventually accepts the song's formulation rather than his or her own?

I play The Replacements' 1987 song "The Ledge" to talk about these questions. The narrator of the song is on the ledge, ready to jump, feeling the power of his position, pledging at the end that the officer trying to reach him won't get a medal. Should radio stations play a song that offers a believable rationale for suicide? What if one person kills himself as a result? What if one thousand people do?

In response to public hand-wringing about popular music's evil effects following the revelations that the Columbine killers and other recent adolescent sociopaths listened to particular rock music, Kevin Dettmar wrote an extended piece on the issue of suicide in rock music and how people who trace suicides to particular lyrics often miss the central irony in the song. While he's no doubt right, Dettmar makes what I consider a fundamental mistake by assuming that people who appropriate pieces of a song do so after making sense of the song itself. He's puzzled about how Kurt Cobain in his suicide note could quote Neil Young's "My My, Hey Hey" about the advantages of burning out young without seeing the irony in the song (Dettmar 2000c). But Cobain had obviously made the line his, with his own meaning, as does everyone who adopts a song line. I think the defense of literate America against the censors should not be "The songs don't really advocate bad things" but "songwriters can't control what listeners are going to make of their lyrics any more than Webster's can control what people do with words in the dictionary."

The social science research generally shows that the cause and effect between music listening and behavior is complex and murky, but Christenson and Roberts report some strong correlations between one type of music and suicidal thoughts. "Clearly, heavy metal music attracts just the sort of youth most likely to be at risk of suicide," they write, and they report on one study that "revealed a strong, positive relationship between [subscriptions to heavy metal magazines] and adolescent suicide" (205). Their wording, however, is crucial—"heavy metal music attracts" certain kinds of kids, not heavy metal *creates* or *causes*. Interestingly, one study showed that Christian heavy metal had the same effects—increasing study participants' negative attitude toward women—as violent heavy metal. "In other words, the lyrics did not make a difference, but the heavy metal musical form did" (209).

I believe that songs can change behavior—I wonder how many people became pacifists as a result of listening to Dylan's antiwar songs?—but that assertion does not put me in the camp with those who want to blame Marilyn Manson for high school massacres or Judas Priest for teenage suicides. If we're going to assign cultural blame for such acts, it would make sense to look at the examples of presidents who prove their manhood or distract attention from other subjects by bombing innocent people. If the country's figurehead solves his problems through senseless violence, why shouldn't the rest of us? And we need to remember that the most famous murderers who said they were inspired by music were the Manson family, and the "inspirational" music—"Helter Skelter"—was penned by that agent of death, despair, and communism, Paul McCartney. Besides, as Marjorie Heins puts it, "the continuing claims that media violence has proven adverse effects enables politicians to obscure known causes of violence, such as poverty and poor education, which they seem largely unwilling to address" (31).

Instead of trying to strangle Marilyn Manson, we should listen to the kids in our lives by listening (in some sense) to their music. Ask most students Why that group? and, after the initial disclaimer ("I don't know"), most will respond in a way that reveals something about their thoughts and their emotional state—by lending you the disc, by articulating something about the band, the music, or their own life, or, perhaps, by refusing, with defensive hostility. We need to learn to use these portholes into our students' lives, not condemn them for existing.

Write: Radical Views of High School

After discussing how different listeners could derive different meanings from so-called suicide songs or how Neil Young could deify a people who had their own very human problems, I like to make sure that students get a chance to go through the process of constructing their own meanings, to see in particular how much control the meaning maker has over the final conclusions about an event. So I ask them to write about a subject familiar to virtually every college student: high school. First, we write for five minutes on our high school experiences, viewing them as failures, presenting a few details that fit the "I was a high school loser" construction. I write mine on the board, usually focusing on the three central concerns of my teenage years— becoming a good wrestler, winning the "highest average" award, and losing my virginity—and detailing my nearly perfect losing record as a wrestler, the school's elimination of my award two weeks before I was going to get it, and my dismal failure socially.

After that depressing five minutes, we write again—same subject, if possible the same details, but now seeing ourselves as successes, "the high school years of the rising star." I stick to the same areas of my life, but now emphasize my nearly perfect wrestling record (as a JV), my triumph over my academic rival (even if they didn't give me a plaque for it), my success at having sex before I graduated.

The discussion afterward is always amusing. I make sure that students understand that what they just did is the essence of therapy, replacing the negative outlooks, the "failure" stories, with more positive ones. And I stress that our ability to achieve such a radical transformation of reality through writing is one reason why writing can be so therapeutic. I ask students which version was easier to write, which seemed more natural; the answers tell us much about our own natural inclinations, our typical outlook on the world. If the negative view is more comfortable and easy, the exercise can display that negativity and leave us with the obvious conclusion that we need to work to tell the more positive story. The exercise demonstrates both the power and the limitations of our ability to construct meaning. There *is* a reality that no wishful thinking can change: I didn't win the wrestling championship. But the conclusions we draw from that reality, the way we feel about it, the way we assess it in our own consciousness *can* change. These conclusions depend very much on who is making the meaning and their beliefs, their assumptions, and even their particular mood on a particular day.

Six

Understanding Voice and Tone

When looking for new singers, producers do not judge a candidate by his repertoire . . . nor, initially, by his technical skills. . . . What they do try to recognize, first and foremost, and to single out wherever possible, is a "voice" . . . the basis for the relationship that must be established between the singer's persona and his songs . . . an indication of one's personality.

Antoine Hennion, "The Production of Success: An Antimusicology of the Pop Song," 1983

It is amazing how much more efficient it is to show . . . with music rather than to try to hammer writing theory in people's minds.

Iren Bencze, grad student, 2002

Throughout this book, I draw many of the insights about teaching writing from analogies with music. Such analogies are nowhere more important than in this chapter, where comparisons to music illuminate some of the most subtle but important elements of writing. Familiarity with music can help students appreciate such things as writing voice and style that, without the analogies, they might dismiss as concerns and techniques for professionals and connoisseurs.

Voice

Voice is easier to hear than to define, whether you're distinguishing between your mother's or your aunt's telephone voices or between the sentence patterns or metaphors used by Virginia Woolf and Flannery O'Connor. It includes elements of style, diction, syntax, register, tone, and persona, but it is more than and different from all those things. Yet it is crucial to good writing; substitute *writer* for *singer* in the opening quotation, and you could mount it on the wall of virtually any magazine or publishing house in America.

Obviously using voice to describe writing is being metaphorical, so one way to spark a discussion of writing voice is to get literal and play human voices, trying to articulate what distinguishes one from another. How can we tell Mel Torme's voice from Mick Jagger's, Janet Jackson's from Ella Fitzgerald's, Lennon's from McCartney's? Is it pitch, accuracy, fullness, the sense of the voice coming from nose, mouth, throat, or chest? If we can decide on one firm distinction—the sense that Ella's voice comes from somewhere deeper, further within, than Janet's, say—does that have an analogue in writing—the difference in depth or resonance between your friend's "great" poem and those of Sharon Olds, for instance?

Digging deep into the attraction of certain voices might yield a lesson in how our taste is constructed. Why does a gruff Howlin' Wolf or Janis Joplin appeal to some of us, a smooth James Taylor or Joan Baez to others? What made Marilyn Monroe's breathy "Happy Birthday Mr. President" sound sexy to so many people? What in Janis Joplin's manner of singing a single word—*roadblock*—makes Big Brother's Monterey Pop Festival song so riveting ("Roadblock")? (And she was only singing backup!)

Almost all students respond to singing voices, but few can articulate their response. They don't have the vocabulary and are often limited to analogy—"kind of like that guy from Green Day but not as snotty." To build that vocabulary and exercise our critical aural skills, I like to extend the metaphor from human utterance to writing—and to electric guitars.

Variations on a Theme by Chuck Berry

Critics and practitioners of rock have long argued that the electric guitar became *the* rock instrument because it is so malleable, so expressive, perhaps the next best thing to the human voice itself. Guitarists have distinctive sounds—produced by unique timings, phrasings, ways of bending notes, of holding the pick, of getting the other fingers of the picking hand into the action—that transcend particular instruments and genres. And because two guitarists sometimes play exactly the same notes—something writers aren't encouraged to do—we can compare guitar "voices" without the distracting variable of melody. Such comparisons can help illuminate what we mean by voice.

To illustrate this phenomenon, I use Chuck Berry's opener, "the most famous musical signature in rock & roll" (Flanagan 1986, 85). I play some original Chuck Berry songs and talk about starting to go to dances in the early 1960s where you could tell when things were really getting cool because the band played Berry's "Johnny B. Goode" or "Roll Over Beethoven" or "Carol." Berry's brand of energy in his speeded-up blues riffs, a new kind of rhythm in the evolution of rhythm and blues, influenced millions of younger musicians, and for years most great rock guitarists at some point in their careers paid homage to the early master. Though he has played many different kinds of music in his long career, Berry, like Elmore James, made a name for himself with variations of a single guitar line that first appeared in "Roll Over Beethoven" and was echoed two years later in "Johnny B. Goode." (In an interview with Bill Flanagan, Berry says he actually borrowed the riff from "Louie Jordon's guitar player, Carl Hogan" [1986, 85].)

Once I've introduced students to the "theme," I start playing variations. I tell students our task is part game show, part study of voice. I invite them to try to guess the group and guitarist, but more important, to come up with words to describe the new voice in comparison to the previous ones. We fill the board with such words, and a surprising number of them have useful analogues in writing—pitch, tone, speed, staccato, flowing, authoritative, loud. Writers and guitarists can be shrill or somber, slow-moving or peppy, rhythmic or jerky. Even words seemingly dedicated to electric guitar talk—like distortion and improvisation—have interesting parallels in writing. Emily Dickinson might have been talking about distortion when she wrote, "Tell all the truth but tell it slant." And improvisation is a goal for many writers who ask, with E. M. Forster, "How do I know what I think until I see what I say?"

Our first stop after Berry's originals is the bright, trebly sound of George Harrison playing lead for the Beatles' version of "Roll Over Beethoven." When I play the Beach Boys' live version of "Johnny B. Goode," the words *busy* or *frenetic* often come up, and when I switch to the much slower, lower intro to the Stones' version of Berry's "Carol," descriptions like *sexy* or even *salacious* sometimes emerge. (Keith Richards would, I'm sure, be proud.)

The next step is usually the most fun, as the same old riff starts playing but with a new sense of authority, assertiveness, and expertise. The class sits silent and stunned until someone risks a tentative "Hendrix?"

We spend a minute trying to pinpoint the source of the authoritativeness, the tone that others have been trying to imitate for thirty years, the guitar voice that some students today can identify even before it expands with distortion and veers off the familiar track into an improvisation that none of the previous guitarists would have imagined.

Johnny Winter has the unenviable job of following Hendrix. Though once promoted as "the Great White Hope of the current blues revival" and given "a record-making $600,000" for signing with Columbia (Goldman), Winter is virtually unknown to students today, but more than once, a student interested in blues has identified Winter's state—Texas—without knowing the musician himself. The sound of Winter's slide guitar has something to do with this regional identification, as does the ferocious, driven quality of the attack. It sounds a bit like a more recent Texas guitar hero, Stevie Ray Vaughan. I'm not enough of an expert to be able to define clearly a Texas sound, but a student's ability to intuit a state's guitar voice can expand the discussion into questions of what elements link our writing to that of others who share our race, gender, or place.

I complete the sixties guitar hero sampler by playing the Grateful Dead doing "Johnny B. Goode," and even students who don't know Jerry Garcia's name often come up with descriptors that reflect his tastes and background—mellow, flowing, country.

We end with Judas Priest. Students recognize the genre—heavy metal or "big hair rock"—almost instantaneously, often with amusement, and it's instructive to probe for the clues that make such identification so easy—the speed, the volume, the aggressive showing off, the (rather ugly, to my ear) attempt to inject a lower, slower "heavy" riff. After I hit the stop button, we apply some of the terms on the board to writing.

With a board full of descriptions of electric guitar "voices," I have students read a paragraph of their own writing—one that feels "like them"—and apply the terms on the board, or others they come up with, to their own voice. (I add new words to the board as we go.) After spending some time analyzing others' voice, students are more open than they would normally be about describing their own writing. Most students (indeed, I would guess, most writers) have only a vague sense of how their voice comes across to others. After struggling to describe their own voice for five minutes, the students exchange paragraphs and describe someone else's, then compare notes.

Finally, the class brainstorms a list of the building blocks of voice, the small elements of writing that, if used in a consistent way, constitute voice: vocabulary, sentence length, sentence structure (including such things as compound or complex versus simple, linear versus embedded, and periodic), sentence type (statement, question, and so on), point of view, use of metaphors, jargon, humor, or slang. I encourage students to experiment with their own voice simply by changing sentence length—cutting sentences into pieces if they tend to write long ones; combining sentences if they lean toward short ones.

Students remember this musical voice exercise better than anything else I do in class. One student wrote, "I find myself telling people about the Johnny B. Goode thing you did all the time . . . It made me think about the components of a song which make it last through the years and how in writing there are other components which make a story timeless. In fact, the idea of story passing from one generation to the next is very intriguing" (Lester). Another, a grad student, said, "Until that lesson, I really never understood what teachers mean by voice . . . ; that lesson has changed the way I write and teach" (Michael Ward).

By the way, if anyone knows of a *female* guitarist who plays Berry's riff, please e-mail me.

Many Voices, One Singer

Another way to make a musical analogy to writing voice is to play the many different voices of a versatile singer. When introducing students to the concept of voice, we need to be careful not to give the impression that each writer has one identifiable, invariant voice. It's more accurate usually to speak of the voice of the particular piece, whether it's an essay or a story. Even a voice as readily identifiable as William Faulkner's varies a good deal from book to book, story to story, from the endless sentences of *Absalom, Absalom!* to the fragmentary internal monologues of *The Sound and the Fury* to the relatively brief narrations of *As I Lay Dying*. This last book is particularly useful for talking about voice, since fifteen different characters narrate their own chapters, and the whole is relatively accessible. What differentiates Vardaman's chapters from Cash's and Darl's? Can we pluck a sentence randomly and identify the narrator? Can we find ways to describe what's common to all the narrations, what we might call Faulkner's voice or the voice of the book, rather than a character's?

The voices of Bob Dylan provide the best musical warm-up for such analysis. In a career now extending into its fifth decade, Dylan has changed approach, genre, and audiences often, several times moving so radically that he left large groups of fans behind. Students, perhaps familiar with his latest releases, might be interested to compare the voice of 2002 with that of 1961. Have forty years made the voice of the sixties generation more gravelly, more raspy, tired, pained, resigned, bitter, mellow? Can they hear all that smoking and singing? Does Dylan's voice still represent his generation—now grandparents, in many cases—or does it retain some of its ability to move the young and rebellious? A more ambitious approach could sample voices from throughout his career, for sometimes Dylan changes more from album to album or even song to song than from decade to decade.

As I've already pointed out in my discussion of "I Want You" (Chapter 4), Dylan's habit of remaking and radically revising his own songs can be extremely valuable for sparking discussions about voice, tone, and style. What differences do students hear between the original 1965 version of "Like a Rolling Stone," perhaps his most famous song, and the live version found on *Self Portrait*? For an exploration of tone, I can't imagine a pair better than the two versions of "Idiot Wind," the one that he chose to release on *Blood on the Tracks* and the earlier-recorded version that appeared decades later on the *Bootleg Series* album. The *Blood* version is, according to the *Bootleg* liner notes, "vengeful, hostile, and bitterly disgusted" (Bauldie, 48), while the *Bootleg* version is more meditative, self-questioning, tentative; "the mood is more of sorrow than anger" (49).

Voice Versus Technique

Voice is inextricably related to technique, but I like to make a distinction between the two, especially with students who think that bigger and more is better. So I play some Yngie Malmsteen. Whenever my friend Stefan, a creative and stylish guitarist, wants to put down a show-off musician, he makes an allusion to "Yngie." Malmsteen, a Swedish guitarist, is blindingly fast, but Stefan isn't the only music listener to think that he embodies the excess of technique over melody, style, and voice. So Malmsteen's is the only music I ever play to criticize, or at least challenge. Does he overdo it? Does he use, as someone once said of Mozart, too many notes?

Most students have no difficulty in agreeing that, yes, Malmsteen overdoes it; few are excited by his brand of heavy metal anyway. Christenson and Roberts found a strong correlation between a taste for heavy metal and a rebellious attitude toward school (104), so most people who make it to college have seen their heavy-metal peers weeded out and have drawn at least a subconscious conclusion about that weeding. At the same time, they may harbor a vague notion that in writing, more is better—more syllables in each word, more adjectives, more adverbs, more metaphors or footnotes or quotations. So playing Malmsteen and talking about excess can lead to a central debate I used to have with MBA students, many of whom were retreating from save-the-world jobs to safe and well-paid positions in business. They wanted their writing to set them apart, to say "this writer is well-educated," and if that meant confusing readers and losing an audience, so be it. They would agree that writing should communicate, but one of the main things they wanted to communicate was how smart they were. The trouble is, in my experience, people trying to prove what great writers they are mostly just reveal their desperation.

Tone

Any musical piece can be the center of a discussion about voice and tone; while most Beethoven and Bach recordings don't have literal voices, the voice of the composer is reasonably consistent throughout the opus—and consistently different from other composers' voices. All great composers use a range of tones, of course, but Beethoven's music certainly has more stormy passages, Bach's more elegant symmetry.

One of the easiest ways to start talking about tones is to play two different versions of the same song. The most radical change in tone I know is Tori Amos' remake of Nirvana's "Smells Like Teen Spirit." What in Nirvana's hands was loud, abrasive, and caustic becomes quiet, beautiful, almost pleading. Another of my favorite pairs: the versions of "Soul Kitchen" by the Doors and X. Both were L.A. bands with tough, confrontational, sexy images. The Doors' song is slow, languorous, sensuous, while even the first few guitar chords of the X version make Jim Morrison and company sound somnambulant, doddering. The slow seduction of the snake is replaced by snappy, insistent double time. It's a demand rather than a plea, and now by a woman, X's Exene Cervenka, not macho Jim Morrison. Any student can hear the difference, and spending a few minutes articulating that difference can add to students' understanding of and vocabulary about tone.

Tone and Persuasion

Some of the most interesting tones to explore are those that break stereotypes and cross common barriers. The antifeminist backlash has gripped many of my students and made them deaf to the virtues of singers like Liz Phair, Polly Jean Harvey, or Corin Tucker of Sleater-Kinney. Listening to some of their lyrics or just reacting to their aggressive tone, many students would immediately dismiss them as *feminazis* or *man haters*. It's certainly worth exploring and challenging such prejudices and reactions, but sometimes I can achieve the same results by having students listen to a feminist message conveyed with a different tone.

Peggy Seeger has a voice unlikely to raise anyone's ire. On her song, "I'm Gonna Be an Engineer," her voice is high, cheerful, feminine, a tad wistful, a voice any conservative young man would be proud to take home to his parents. But anyone who listens to the lyrics realizes that that sweet voice can convey anger, bitterness, and the kind of determination that leaves some listeners cheering with tears in their eyes (see Figure 6–1). The singer is going to be an engineer, despite having to put her husband through school, despite getting paid much less than a man, despite running into prejudice and condescension everywhere she turns in her chosen profession. By the end of the song, she is asserting that she is a "damn good" engineer and vowing to "fight" to be recognized. It's a strident message, but the tone makes it palatable. And analyzing the tone can help students both become sharper readers and learn how to be more persuasive— less offensive—writers. Every writer who wants to write persuasively needs to learn the lesson from Seeger's song—a strident message can be delivered in a tone that invites the listener or the reader to think and ponder rather than reject the message out of hand.

Humor

Just as the right tone can make almost any idea inoffensive, humor can help convey almost any message. Music with a humorous edge rewards analysis because it's fun to listen to and because its success often depends on tone, as well as on knowledge shared by singer and listener. Weird Al Yankovic has made a career out of singing parodies of other people's songs, and currently popular groups like Ween, They Might Be Giants, and Barenaked Ladies owe some of their following to their ability to make people laugh about subjects from the silly to the serious.

Romantic Irony

All the performers mentioned in the previous paragraph use *romantic irony,* one of my favorite analytical terms because it validates a double reaction that many readers have to literature and other art forms— we're drawn in, persuaded, romantically caught up, yet at the same time we view with irony, perhaps humor. I was first introduced to the term by G. R. Thompson in his book, *Poe's Fiction: Romantic Irony in the Gothic Tales*, in which he argued, "We can respond to Poe's scenes of horror or despair at the same time that we are aware of their caricatural quality" (14). He makes sense of the common feeling among readers that Poe's writing can be both deliciously and ridiculously overwrought.

I help students latch on to the concept by playing a song from the album *Cruising with Ruben and the Jets*, in which Frank Zappa and the Mothers of Invention take on the personae of a 1950s doo-wop group. "Stuff Up the Cracks" is a farcical tragedy about a man who's going to turn on the gas one last time if his lover leaves him. Despite the silly lyrics and whiny vocals, the musicians take the music seriously, and the last minute of the song is a startling Zappa guitar solo, a bit of cutting-edge late-sixties fusion that somehow develops naturally from the plodding fifties tune. We laugh but we listen intently to what Frederick Jameson calls "a systematic mimicry of . . . deliberate eccentricities" (65). Once again, we use music to complicate students' thinking, to move away from simple labels and dichotomies, to show that *both/and* is both possible and sometimes intriguing. As Billy Corgan of the Smashing Pumpkins put it, "Not only do we respect the clichés, we see truth in them. So we simultaneously make fun of them and embrace them" (quoted in Obstfeld and Fitzgerald, 71).

Sarcasm

"Kill kill kill the poor," Jello Biafra sings on the Dead Kennedys' first album, *Fresh Fruit for Rotting Vegetables*. The band's name alone provokes public outrage, and their songs can demonstrate that extreme of irony and tone, sarcasm.

I warn my students that any type of humor is difficult to convey successfully in writing and sarcasm probably the most difficult. I advise against trying it. But I still like to talk about it on occasion, and "Kill the Poor" provides a perfect example. "Efficiency and progress is ours once more," Biafra sings with apparent pride, "Now that we have the Neutron bomb." The song paints attractive pictures of the future without slums and "jobless millions"; rich whites will have "more room to play."

Once students hear the catchy chorus—"Kill kill kill kill kill the poor"—they'll find themselves singing along and then stop, embarrassed, and think about the implications of what they're singing. I suppose it would be possible for someone to read or hear the words as serious; white supremacist groups no doubt have said and written crazier things. If they're not convinced the song is sarcastic, a quick dose of context—mentioning some of the other song titles, for instance, like "Let's Lynch the Landlord"—should bring them around. And then we can discuss what makes sarcasm work. In this case I think one of the lessons is that the words in question *could* be serious; some people really would like to use a neutron bomb to "clean up" the cities and make more room for the rich. That edge of uncertainty may increase the effect of the joke, but student writers need to think about how difficult it is to steer between the exaggerated sneering sarcasm of their younger siblings and the totally ambiguous, too-subtle sarcasm of writers who assume everyone feels as they do.

Write: Fifteen Minutes of Faulkner

To create a kind of written analogue to the Chuck Berry guitar parade, I give the whole class the same material to work with and then listen for the different voices as they read what they've made out of the shared materials. We start with thirty bits of information (mostly individual *T-units*, to use the grammatical jargon, though any grammarian will note that my units are neither parallel nor consistent) that I took from a famous sentence—the first sentence of William Faulkner's *Absalom, Absalom!* (see Figure 6–2). I ask everyone to combine the information in whatever way appeals to them. Sometimes I encourage them to write as few sentences as possible, to approximate the original; sometimes I leave the combining entirely up to them. Then we read our productions aloud, compare our versions to Faulkner's original (Figure 6–3), and try to identify distinguishing elements in each, elements that define individual voices. If possible, we use the terms still on the board from the Chuck Berry voice exercise. None of us can be William Faulkner, just as none of us can be Chuck Berry, but we can still enjoy listening to the personalities emerge from different interpretations of their music.

I use a variation of this exercise to assess and, if necessary, grade student ability to build tight grammatical sentences. Having everyone start with the same material eliminates the subject matter variable from writing assessment; craft alone creates the differences between one student's paragraph and another's. I take a paragraph from an encyclopedia—one on barbed wire is my favorite—and break it into small pieces for students to combine. See the work of William Strong (*Coaching Writing* is his most recent book) for scores of more sophisticated uses of sentence combining.

Figure 6–1

I'm Gonna Be an Engineer

When I was a little girl, I wished I was a boy
I tagged along behind the gang and wore me corduroys
Everybody said I only did it to annoy
But I was gonna be an engineer
    Mama told me "Can't you be a lady?
    Your duty is to make me the mother of a pearl
    Wait until you're older dear and maybe
    You'll be glad that you're a girl"
        Dainty as a Dresden Statue
        Gentle as a Jersey cow
        Smooth as silk, gives creamy milk
        Learn to coo, learn to moo
        That's what you do to be a lady now

When I went to school I learned to write and how to read
Some history, geography and home economy
And typing is a skill that every girl is sure to need
To while away the extra time until the time to breed
And then they had the nerve to say, "What would you like to be?"
I says "I'm gonna be an engineer!"
    No, you only need to learn to be a lady
    The duty isn't yours for to try and run the world
    An engineer could never have a baby!
    Remember, dear, that you're a girl
        She's smart! for a woman
        I wonder how she got that way?
        You get no choice, you get no voice
        Just stay mum, pretend you're dumb
        That's how you come to be a lady today!

So I become a typist and I study on the sly
Working out the day and night so I can qualify
And every time the boss come in he pinched me on the thigh
Says "I've never had an engineer!"
    You owe it to the job to be a lady
    It's the duty of the staff to give the boss a whirl
    The wages that you get are crummy maybe
    But it's all you get 'cause you're a girl

Then Jimmy come along and we set up a conjugation
We were busy every night with loving recreation
I spent my day at work so HE could get his education
And now he's an engineer!
    He says "I know you'll always be a lady
    It's the duty of me darling to love me all her life
    Could an engineer look after or obey me?
    Remember, dear, that you're my wife"

Well as soon as Jimmy got a job, I began again
Then happy at me turret-lathe a year or so and then
The morning that the twins were born, Jimmy says to them
"Kids, your mother WAS an engineer"
     You owe it to the kids to be a lady
     Dainty as a dish-rag, faithful as a chow
     Stay at home, you got to mind the baby
     Remember you're a mother now

Well everytime I turn around it's something else to do
It's cook a meal or mend a sock or sweep a floor or two
I listen in to Jimmy Young, it makes me want to spew
I was gonna be an engineer!
     I really wish that I could be a lady
     I could do the lovely things that a lady's 'sposed to do
     I wouldn't even mind if only they would pay me
     And I could be a person too
          What price—for a woman?
          You can buy her for a ring of gold
          To love and obey (without any pay)
          You get a cook and a nurse (for better or worse)
          You don't need a purse when a lady is sold

Ah but now that times are harder and me Jimmy's got the sack
I went down to Vicker's, they were glad to have me back
But I'm a third-class citizen, my wages tell me that
And I'm a first-class engineer
     The boss he says "We pay you as a lady
     You only got the job 'cause I can't afford a man
     With you I keep the profits high as may be
     You're just a cheaper pair of hands"
          You got one fault: you're a woman
          You're not worth the equal pay
          A bitch or a tart, you're nothing but heart
          Shallow and vain, you got no brain
          You even go down the drain like a lady today

Well I listened to my mother and I joined a typing pool
I listened to my lover and I put him thru his school
But if I listen to the boss, I'm just a bloody fool
And an underpaid engineer!
     I been a sucker ever since I was a baby
     As a daughter, as a wife, as a mother and a "dear"
     But I'll fight them as a woman, not a lady
     I'll fight them as an engineer!

Figure 6–2

Combine all these details into sentences of your own creation.

1. They sat from a little after two oclock until almost sundown.
2. It was September.
3. It was a hot afternoon.
4. It was a weary afternoon.
5. It was a long afternoon.
6. It was a still afternoon.
7. Miss Coldfield was one of them.
8. They sat in a room.
9. Miss Coldfield called the room the office.
10. Miss Coldfield's father called the room the office.
11. Miss Coldfield took after her father in using the term the office.
12. The room was dim.
13. The room was hot.
14. The room was airless.
15. All the blinds were closed.
16. All the blinds were fastened.
17. The blinds had been kept the same way for 43 summers.
18. The blinds were kept the same way because of someone's belief.
19. The blinds had been kept that way since she was a girl.
20. Someone believed that light and moving air carried heat.
21. Someone believed that dark was always cooler.
22. As the sun shone fuller and fuller on that side of the house, something happened.
23. The room became latticed with yellow slashes.
24. The yellow slashes were full of motes.
25. The motes were made of dust.
26. Quentin thought of the motes as being flecks of the paint.
27. The paint was old, dried.
28. Wind might have blown the flecks inward.
29. The flecks might have been from the blinds.
30. The blinds were scaling.

Figure 6–3

From *Absalom, Absalom!* by William Faulkner (1936)

From a little after two oclock until almost sundown of the long still hot weary dead September afternoon they sat in what Miss Coldfield still called the office because her father had called it that—a dim hot airless room with the blinds all closed and fastened for forty-three summers because when she was a girl someone had believed that light and moving air carried heat and that dark was always cooler, and which (as the sun shone fuller and fuller on that side of the house) became latticed with yellow slashes full of dust motes which Quentin thought of as being flecks of the dead old dried paint itself blown inward from the scaling blinds as wind might have blown them.

Seven

Constructing Genres

*[Adults] have often been amazed at the degree to which ado-
lescents can detect subtle nuances among substyles within
popular music.*
       Janet R. Barrett, Claire W. McCoy, and Kari K. Veblen,
                                Sound Ways of Knowing, 1997

*"I don't want to kiss you / I don't want to touch," the narrator of
Elvis Costello's "No Action" sings. We may initially accept his
denials, his lack of interest, but when he starts getting excited about
"inserting [his] coin" and praises himself for disconnecting in time,
we no longer believe him. He is, as any student can recognize, an
unreliable narrator. He may be an interesting character to follow,
and we may enjoy the story he tells and the way he tells it, but we
don't trust him or his story.*

*By playing a couple of minutes of music and distributing some
simple lyrics, we can help students understand a concept that's central
to modern fiction. Having encountered, enjoyed, and developed suspi-
cions about an unreliable narrator in a song, students are more ready
to identify such narrators in Faulkner or Nabokov or Erdrich, to label
their unreliability, and to appreciate their narratives. This chapter
focuses on ways to use music to make such points, to help define genres and techniques and ease students toward an understanding of
some of the technical aspects of written genres.*

*Because song lyrics are a cousin to both fiction and poetry, they
share a number of techniques, terms, and concepts. Since song lyrics
tend to be simpler and shorter than most short stories and poems, it's*

easier to see and understand these writing elements when we focus on
lyrics. We can teach much of the technical side of any genre by intro-
ducing it with musical examples rather than literary ones.

Poetry

I imagine that many teachers who bring song lyrics into the classroom
do so to consider some variation of the question, Are song lyrics poetry? It's a reasonable question: lyrics and poetry share certain features—line breaks, stanza form, compression, sometimes rhythm and
rhyme, often figures of speech. I certainly support teachers who
examine lyrics to a Liz Phair or Radiohead song as they would a
poem.[1] Such examinations might most logically focus on the lyrics of
Jim Carroll, Leonard Cohen, or Patti Smith, since all three were published poets before they became singers and lyricists.

Throughout this book, I advocate approaching song lyrics with the
tools of poetic analysis, so that students can try out their terms, practice their parsing, study their syllabication with songs. But after years
of asking the "lyrics = poetry?" question, I finally came to the conclusion that I don't like the question itself; it implies a hierarchical
approach to the written arts that I don't buy. When we ask, Is it poetry? we usually mean, Is it good enough to be poetry?, and that question obviously implies that poetry as a genre is superior to song lyrics
as a genre. Popular culture is by definition inferior to high culture.

The weight and universality of that kind of judgment have always
been difficult for supporters of popular culture to shrug off. So we
tend to defend song lyrics by saying, "Well, yeah, some of the good
ones *are* good enough to be poetry." And making that claim often
seems radical enough. But after several repetitions, that defense starts
sounding like an insult, as though someone were saying yes, some
black folks are good enough to be considered white, or yes, some top
women can compete with the average man. We seldom ask, "Could
that poem make it as a song?" And we forget the relationship of lyrics
to the song: as Pete Seeger put it, "the printed lyrics of folk songs [are]
like a photograph of a bird in flight" (Leland, 39).

We can see the assumed inferiority of rock music in the excitement generated by any bit of rock that has pretensions to a "higher,"
classical form, something more serious than, "above," the rock norm.
That's one of the reasons, I think, that *Sgt. Pepper*, something of a *concept* album but far from the Beatles' best, gets so much press, and that
a rock opera like the Who's *Tommy* caused such a stir. Such albums
toyed with intellectual concepts and classical forms; they gave traditional music critics something familiar to respond to. Maybe if Rage

Against the Machine wrote lyrics in the form of sonnets, they too would get serious critical attention.

So now, while I might play Joni Mitchell's "Both Sides Now" and discuss some of its poetic features, I don't ask if it should be considered poetry. Instead, I explain my stance on the issue and ask students about the hierarchy of genres in their own minds and where it came from. Why *do* we often put poetry on the top of the heap? And why do we value fiction over nonfiction, short stories over newspaper articles? I don't have any solid answers to such questions, but I imagine English teachers bear some of the blame, and we clearly need to fight against the popular impression that only certain kinds of readings are sanctioned or legitimate. Difficult novels have more cachet than Harlequin romances for some good reasons, but we need to articulate those reasons, not let students think that our preferences are just prejudices.

Teachers who don't care about such theoretical issues, however, can have great fun with the is-it-poetry? question. One of my ex-students, now a teacher, e-mailed me about giving out the lyrics to Simon and Garfunkel's "I Am a Rock."

> I asked them whether or not they thought what I had given them was a poem. They all decided it was . . . I asked all of them to bring in a song that they thought was a poem. Boy, the next class period we listened to everything from Garth Brooks to *Les Misérables*. The students were really excited to share their music with the rest of the class. Also, discussing terms like *alliteration* and *metaphor* was much easier for the students when they were able to look at their own "poems" rather than a poem I selected for them.
>
> We had just finished a unit on Steinbeck's *Of Mice and Men* and discussed how loneliness was a theme in the book, so this song tied into our discussion of how we, as humans, need or do not need some kind of companionship. [Also] the similes, metaphors, rhyme patterns, etc., are easy to recognize so when we started discussing these terms I had concrete examples for the students to refer to. (Moody-Bouwhuis)

Clearly the value in such an exercise is not in reaching an answer to the question Is it poetry? but in finding an amusing way to examine, define, describe, and use the elements of sound, rhythm, metaphor, and diction that constitute poetry.

Taste and "Good" Writing

Disrupting the house of cards that is the traditional hierarchy of value in English raises the extremely tricky issue of judging and evaluating any written product. If a poem isn't necessarily better than a news story, does that mean we must give up on all measures of value, all judgment, and simply accept writing as writing? I find the question of valuing writing, especially poetry, to be very difficult, but we have to face it or risk allowing students to come to their own conclusions about value in writing: "It's just what the teacher likes" or "If you meant what you said, then no one can say it's not good."

The only way I've found to deal satisfactorily with the issue of taste is to get students involved in defining *good* writing. Either as a whole or in groups, the class first brainstorms the elements of good writing, usually expressed as full sentences: "The paper has a point." "The sentences are grammatical." Once we've gathered a daunting number of sentences, we look for categories into which we can group and perhaps conflate several ideas—*mechanics, focus, sentences,* and so on. I assign each group one of these categories, and each group combines and rephrases the sentences in its category, working to cover the category as completely as possible in a few concise sentences. Throughout this process, I sprinkle in suggestions of issues the class might want to consider, trying to avoid big gaps in the final list.

Finally, the groups reform as a class and put their results on the board for further refining by the class as a whole. I type up our extended definition and distribute it for the next class period. Even students who would argue that taste is totally subjective usually have no trouble coming up with "objective" criteria; they've all had years of training, being told what's right and wrong in their English classes. And by the time we finish fine-tuning, we usually manage to make our statements sensible and relevant.

We can't fully answer the question of taste with this exercise, and inevitably some students have trouble seeing the motes in their own papers. But for most students, the process of formulating their own definition develops loyalty to and responsibility for that opinion, and the list provides a powerful communication tool for any further discussion of taste, value, and grades. At its best, this process, in McNamee's words, "invite[s] others into generative and transformative conversations where we create what counts as knowledge together"; "as we engage with each other we not only create a sense of who we are but also a sense of what is valued." That sense may be the best outcome of this kind of exercise.

Bennett Reimer suggests an alternative approach to developing guidelines for taste and aesthetic judgments. His framework for judgment involves four categories: craftsmanship, sensitivity, imagination, and authenticity (332–36). I find some of his category names confusing, and he takes what I consider to be an outmoded stance, assuming that the qualities he's interested in reside in the work itself and not in some kind of relationship between the work and the reader/listener. He writes that "sensitivity . . . has to do with the depth and quality of feeling captured in the dynamic form of a work" (333). About imagination, he says, "Every good work of art . . . must have enough originality to vivify our feelings" (335). And while he begins his definition of authenticity by saying that it "raises the issue of morality," he's using *morality* to talk about a work's "fidelity to its inner needs" (337), not about the kind of morality promoted by the family values movement. Nor is he interested in the kind of authenticity that Simon Frith sees in the strain in Bruce Springsteen's face as he sings "We Are the World": "authenticity . . . guaranteed by visible physical effort" (1987, 147).

In spite of these quibbles, I find his four concepts compelling and perhaps useful for class. For ease of student understanding, I might call them something like *craft, depth of feeling, originality,* and *internal consistency.* Although judgments in each of these categories are obviously subjective, having students focus on their own beliefs and values about each category might make the issues of taste and aesthetic judgment seem less hopelessly individual and idiosyncratic.

Genre Boundaries and Their Value

How does fidelity to genre enter into discussions about quality and taste? Do we value the sonnet or the blues song that perfectly follows the traditional form, or are we more impressed by originality and departures from the form? Examining genres and their boundaries can help us develop our own answers to such questions and in the process explore our own tastes.

I like opening a class with Peter, Paul, and Mary's version of "If I Had My Way" and asking students who it is. Grateful Dead fans may recognize the rocking tune as one the Dead played for years under the title "Samson and Delilah" and I think most students are surprised to find that the song and the group are "folk," not folk-rock. If they know Peter, Paul, and Mary at all, it's as oldies whom grandparents watch on public TV specials. Why is the song folk, and what would make it rock?

Teachers who want to use a musical entry into the tricky world of genre might be smart to turn to students for help. Ask students to define and distinguish between rap, hip-hop, techno, house, acid, trance, and all other musical genre terms too new for old fogies to understand. Moving back in time, we could talk about what defined grunge. Was it a hybrid or something unique without obvious generic parents?

Any such discussion inevitably reaches the question What's the point in labeling genres at all, if the boundaries are so fuzzy, the definitions so loose? Many of my students, with fresh memories of high school cliques and demeaning high school labels, advocate throwing out labels entirely, treating each individual as unique. So we must detail the value of labels: they help us to find the right area of the CD store, they allow us to communicate quickly ("He's a folkie with a punk rocker inside"), they enable the CD club to send us the right advertising flyer. They allow listeners to locate themselves on various musical continua—hard to soft, instrumental to vocal, old to new.

Most important, genre labels and the information they convey help us understand, perhaps even applaud, the difference in the sameness. If we expect the first two lines to be identical, or the song to be twelve bars long, those repetitive features of blues won't bother us, any more than a fancier of Mozart string quartets would find the similarity of instrumentation a problem. Experience with a genre allows appreciation of that genre; whether you're a mystery novel reader or into gangsta rap, your ability to make predictions, put each new example of the genre into context, and identify subtle variations on a theme allows you to delight in innovations invisible to non-aficionados. Serious listeners and readers know this, and many go out of their way to learn more about their chosen genres to increase their enjoyment, but our students may never have pondered how experience and information can enhance pleasure.

To help them see that they *do* value genre labels, ask them if anyone has ever said of their favorite type of music, "It all sounds the same." That annoying comment has been uttered about every imaginable genre from classical to rap. I remember being particularly provoked when a fellow student, trying to impress our British professor, said it of one of the long blues on Derek and the Dominos' *Layla*, considered by many to be the greatest electric blues record ever made. In a way she was right, of course; the musical and lyrical patterns of the blues are simple and repetitive. *Layla*'s "Key to the Highway" does sound similar to "Have You Ever Loved a Woman?" But on a high enough level of generalization, the same can be said of any two pieces of Mozart, or any two symphonies. Students are almost certain to have heard a similar complaint from parents if not from peers, and they can probably tell you why it's not valid. And by defending the differences in the sameness of various examples of their genre, they at least implicitly defend the concept and value of genre itself.

Even if students reject the advantages of labels, they may take from the discussion a more sophisticated understanding of what we mean when we say that genres are constructs created by writers, critics, readers, and teachers, each of their cookie cutters carving out a slightly different section of the literary dough. Many professors and writing books would like to claim that some forms are fixed, inviolate, and therefore iterations of them are either right or wrong, but they're seldom able to reconcile that view with the fact that the professor in the next office, or the next book on the shelf, is equally certain that a slightly different form is the ideal formal report, literature review, or resume. Students are not well served if they come out of our classes thinking they know *the* way to conceive of and execute a particular writing genre. They'll be better off if they're aware that, for instance, the Fulbright selection committee and Murphy's Greenhouse might judge an application letter by different criteria.

Hybrid Vigor

In both music and writing, some of the most interesting work refuses to be limited by genre boundaries. If we really want to pursue and encourage high quality, we have to be ready to deal with art that doesn't fit easily under any genre labels, some of which borrows from two or more established genres.

This section title refers to a general biological principle (*heterosis*): first-generation hybrids tend to be vigorous growers. Some in the field of English, particularly Tom Romano, who champions the multigenre research paper, are waking the rest of us up to the value of writing that crosses genre boundaries. Often the "vigor" is a function of the tension between the genres; Louise Erdrich's *Love Medicine* fascinates readers in part because the individual sections when read as chapters take on different meanings and emphases than when they're read as independent short stories. Tori Amos' version of "Smells Like Teen Spirit" gets its energy from the tension between the song's grunge origins—ferocious guitars and middle-finger attitude—and Amos' decidedly ungrungy treatment of it.

Some readers, critics, and teachers object to generic cross-dressing and want students to have a clearly defined sense of the distinctions between fiction and nonfiction, between poetry and prose, between novel and short story collection. Perhaps such an attitude is useful in the early grades, when students are learning to understand, appreciate, and define written genres. But I'm more interested in students perceiving that genres are constructs, labels that are useful for communicating about a text but limiting, since they seldom contain all the elements of a given text. Lauryn Hill's music won Grammys precisely because it crosses so many musical boundaries. Of course a song like "When It Hurts So Bad" has some hip-hop in its veins and some late-nineties rhythm and blues, but at times when listening to it, I hear Billie Holiday, with the Vandellas singing Thelonious Monk harmonies in response.

The history of rock is full of hybrids: blues rock, folk rock, country rock, art rock, pop punk, fusion. Each hybrid included some groundbreaking music, and each raised questions that show how tenuous the categories are. Why was the Byrd's version of "Mr. Tambourine Man" considered folk-rock, but Dylan's original wasn't? Does Dylan tend to arouse so much ire—as he did in 1965 when he returned to the electric guitar he'd put down in 1960—because he refuses to hybridize, but instead stays within the genre, producing, for instance, a true country (not country rock) album, *Nashville Skyline*? What recent hybrids—metal rap comes to mind—have the longevity and stability to become accepted genres on their own?

Scorned Genres

Hybrids aren't the only genres that trouble English teachers and music critics. Every era and every discipline has its scorned genres, whether free verse, free-form jazz, or fantasy. Young people don't necessarily *choose* genres to upset or annoy their elders; as Christenson and Roberts put it, "we believe many teens pursue adult-disapproved personal styles and music preferences less to offend or distance themselves from adults than to cultivate a public image of rebelliousness and independence" (60). Whatever the motivation, genre choices almost inevitably drive a wedge between generations. Anyone wanting to bridge that divide can start by examining scorned genres, those that adults, authorities, virtuosos love to hate.

Punk

"God Save the Queen," Johnny Rotten of the Sex Pistols sneers before lobbing the word *fascist* at Her Majesty.

I remember well when I first became conscious of punk rock, because I was already, as I saw it, a rock 'n' roll old-timer by then, I had an unerring sense of taste, and I knew that something that announced itself via fashion statements—bobby pins through cheeks and studded leather—and news spots (about the public's outrage at the Pistols' lyrics and actions) could not be good. What bullshit, I thought, music as a fashion accessory, morons hurting themselves, and I joined the other 99.99 percent of Americans who treated (and for the most part still treat) punk as a bad joke that inexplicably won't die.

With the help of students who insisted I listen to the Pistols, X, and the Ramones, I learned to appreciate the punk sound and ignore the accessorizing. Twenty years later, I feel that I was born a decade too early and should have passed my adolescence singing "I Wanna Be Sedated" with the Ramones. But remembering that early scorn reminds me of how easily superiority masks ignorance, and I try to avoid making the same mistake again. I've learned not so much to modify my opinions as to accept that they may evolve. And while I can't make my students' opinions evolve, I play enough music that I used to hate to let them know that I think evolution is a good thing.

Fantasy

In Chapter 1, I mention a student of mine from the early 1980s who reviewed Cream's *Wheels of Fire*. As we talked about the album, I made the disconcerting discovery that we liked it for opposite reasons—I was fond of the long, live instrumental jams, while Dave preferred studio cuts like "Pressed Rat and Warthog" that wander into fantasy, silliness, or both. I had always considered those songs too precious, the silliness detracting from the music, the allure of the fantasy inexplicable.

But Dave's interest tuned me into what has since become a flood of adolescent fascination with fantasies, fictions that don't pretend to have one foot in reality. With roots in Tolkien, King Arthur, and perhaps Ken Kesey's Merry Pranksters, fantasy rock has been particularly popular in Britain, where groups like Yes made albums with song titles like "Siberian Khatru" and album covers that looked like Tolkien's world warped by psychedelics. Although I like Yes' music, I still have trouble getting excited about fantasy, whether it's a Rush song or the books and video games that absorb much of my eleven-year-old's time.

But I'm convinced that we have to do more in English courses to connect with our students on what they do read, what they do have enthusiasm for. If fantasies about heroic sword-wielding mice and badgers excite them, so be it. We need to exploit the energy that our students invest in traditionally scorned genres—not just sci-fi and fantasy, but the cheesy, the painfully trite, the repulsively romantic. Tom Newkirk makes a strong argument that English teachers need to get off their high horses and admit that sentimentality is a favorite genre among the reading public. And deal with it.

Having been schooled in snooty English classes, I didn't discover that Tolkien was a great storyteller until I read the Hobbit books to my son. But by playing "Pressed Rat" or Phish's "Guyute," I can open a door to that world and see if students are interested in exploring it.

Dreams

If there's one kind of paper or story that English teachers hate even more than fantasy, it's the "dream" story, ending with the inevitable "and then I woke up." Such stories break all the rules of realism, verisimilitude, cause and effect, consistency of time, place, and character. They're a cheap and easy way to avoid the rigors of character development, pacing, or transitions.

But popular music, and in particular folk, has used dreams to convey everything from thinly disguised lust (the Everly Brothers' "All I Have to Do Is Dream") to strident political messages and postapocalyptic hope. Written in 1938 by Alfred Hayes and Earl Robinson and brought to baby boomers by Joan Baez at Woodstock, the folk classic "Joe Hill" is a dream song about the resurrection of Hill, who was executed in Salt Lake City in 1915 because, according to the song, his union organizing activities angered mining companies. In a classroom, "Joe Hill" might, as the song and movie about Hurricane Carter (Dylan) did, lead students to examine their assumptions about innocence and guilt, capital punishment, and the potential malevolence of the state and its police.

One of Dylan's many dream songs, "I Dreamed I Saw St. Augustine," achieves some of its eerie power by echoing "Joe Hill" and could spark a discussion about using historical figures in writing. But for class use, Dylan's "Talkin' World War III Blues" is my favorite dream. The young Dylan sounds like a hillbilly to modern students, and the song could be taken as a joke, but in the end it packs as much punch as any more traditional, coherent song. The dreaming Bob finds himself the only survivor of World War III. His psychiatrist tells him that everyone's been having the same dream, except that of course the sole survivor is different in each one. At the end of the song, Dylan makes an offer, seemingly to his audience, that could stand as a motto for everything that's been good in postwar American culture—the civil rights movement, the peace movement, the women's movement, the environmental movement: "I'll let you be in my dream if I can be in yours."

In the right hands, even the most hopeless genres become fresh. So our job as English teachers should be not to shore up the walls of the citadel to keep out the latest assault on good taste but to learn about what students want to do so we can help them do it well, for instance to use the dream genre to say something rather than to escape the writer's responsibilities.

Refining Genres

The genre we teach most is the essay, and students often arrive in our classes knowing all about it. Because, as Angelo and Cross say, "it's much harder for students to unlearn incorrect or incomplete knowledge than to master new knowledge in an unfamiliar field" (132), I spend a lot of energy shaking lose students' essay habits, trying to open up the possibilities of the form, to get students away from slavish adherence to the thesis-driven five-paragraph essay that presents its conclusion, supports it, and then concludes once again. I don't want to substitute one formula for another, so I don't say "an essay must do this, this, and this," but students often have a difficult time casting off old forms if they have no clue about new ones.

Greg Brown's "If I Had Known" is the most useful song I know for shaking up ideas about essays (Figure 7–1). Brown's narrator tells his story in three segments. After the first two scenes, he concludes that if he had known what lay ahead, he would have stopped doing the activity—fishing in the first scene, kissing in the second—after the first incomparable time, because "things'll never be that good again." It's a convincing, if somewhat depressing outlook. Any listener can probably think of things that would have been better done just once.

But then in the third verse, the narrator describes (in general enough terms for sensitive students) his first sexual experience, this time concluding that knowing what lay ahead would have led him to repeat the experience over and over, since "some things just get better and better, better than they've already been."

It's an intriguing way to set up an essay: disarm the opposing side by presenting impressive evidence for that side, then play the trump card, making the previous conclusion look tentative and now, well, naive. The approach certainly won't work for every essay—and I wouldn't want students to try it too often—but it's a departure from the standard linear form, an approach that some students might enjoy imitating. And the success of such a nonstandard but structured "essay" should help break students' (and teachers') reliance on the five-paragraph formula.

Illuminating Terms and Concepts

Music can help us teach the minutia of genre, the terms and concepts, as well as the larger issues of definition and evolution. I began this chapter demonstrating how Elvis Costello's "No Action" can lead students to understand the concept of unreliable narrator, and I'm convinced that a creative teacher can bring alive almost any term or technique with music. For instance, Vincent A. Lankewish teaches his students about dramatic monologues—as well as authorial distance—by studying Suzanne Vega's "Luka," a monologue by an abused boy. And I'm sure I'm not the only one who uses classical music to discuss *theme* and *thesis*. Students often see thesis as a single sentence that can be glued onto the beginning or end of an essay and somehow infuse focus and organization throughout the whole piece. To complicate that definition and provide a different model of theme and thesis, I play the final movement of Beethoven's Ninth Symphony and ask students to listen to the "joyful, joyful, we adore thee" theme, which is familiar enough and obvious enough for them to pick out easily. They can hear how the theme is repeated with endless variations, tossed from chorus to orchestra and back again, and, because there's enough else going on and the theme itself is interesting, it doesn't seem dull and repetitive. We can't do exactly the same thing in writing essays, but the "Ode to Joy" provides an ideal that we can point to, an example of how a theme can be woven or suffused so it's integral to the whole. After a discussion about their paper in which they've finally fixed on some kind of focus, young writers ask, "Can I just add this idea in the last paragraph?"

"Think about how Beethoven did it" is one kind of answer.

Write: Return to High School

Genre varies with purpose, audience, and a host of other factors, and changing one or two of these factors while working on the same subject can provide good hands-on lessons about writing. As an introduction to such lessons, we can speculate about how and why the Doors' slow-moving psychedelia transformed into driving punk (see Chapter 6), or about why Dylan took the bounce out of "I Want You" and made it into a plaintive lament (see Chapter 4).

I use a number of different approaches to connect such musical genre experiments with student writing. Sometimes I turn to *The Craft of Revision,* in which Donald Murray outlines a number of different forms that a job applicant's message could take and then chooses among them based on the audience's needs (2001a, 107–10). His example can lead students through a similar process, writing about their college prospects to a number of different audiences.

Another option is to follow up the high school exercise at the end of Chapter 5 with some writing exercises based on the same materials. Students can write letters, memos, stories, or poems about a particular high school experience or theme. I ask students to choose at least two different audiences and address each in whatever way seems appropriate. They're free to make up their own audience, but I provide suggestions: your high school principal, an old high school buddy or enemy, a favorite or least favorite teacher, the local school board, yourself at age fifteen, an eighth grader about to enter your high school. Students choose what genre would best suit their audiences, write, and share. They almost always enjoy the exercise, both because it gives them a chance to articulate long-standing, strongly held feelings and because they appreciate the opportunity to choose their own genre rather than stuff their ideas into a genre the teacher has chosen.

Note

1. See Chapter 2 for more on this question. Several of the contributors to "Words and Music" make excellent use of lyrics for studying poetry, and one, Mary Ann Black, uses songs by Rush, Tangerine Dream, and Jethro Tull to lead students into discussing British Romantic poetry.

Figure 7–1

If I Had Known

Greg Brown (1990)

A little creek you could spit across
Jimmy and me each took one more toss
our spinners bright in the evening air
People always said, There ain't no fish in there
Well grownups they ain't always right
Jimmy and me walked home slow that night
right down Main Street in our P.F. Fliers
with two 5 lb. bass making grown men liars

Jimmy if I had known—
I might have stopped fishing right then
It's just as well we don't know
when things will never be that good again

A hayride on an Autumn night
Well we was 15 if I remember right
We were far apart at the start of the ride
but somehow we ended up side by side
We hit a bump and she grabbed my arm
The night was as cold as her lips were warm
I shivered as her hand held mine
And then I kissed her one more time

And Jane if I had known—
I might have stopped kissing right then
It's just as well we don't know
when things will never be that good again

She was older than me I guess
Summer was invented for her to wear that dress
I knew about risk and she knew about proof
and that night she took me up on the roof
We could see the lights of the little towns
We could watch the August stars come down
Shooting stars, meteorites—
we went on a ride through the sky that night

And, oh, if I had known—
I'd do it all over again
Some things just get better and better
and better than they've already been

Eight

Process
Rehearsals, Beginnings, Revisions

The success of a song depends on the accumulation of minor details.
Anonymous music producer quoted in
Antoine Hennion's "The Production of Success:
An Antimusicology of the Pop Song," 1983

I usually rewrite songs for a long time, sometimes for years. I keep trying to uncover what it is I am trying to say. I know that if I stop too soon I'll end up with slogans.
Leonard Cohen, quoted in *Jabberrock*, 1995

"Are You a Boy, or Are You a Girl?" the Barbarians taunted in 1966. A couple of years later, Jefferson Airplane asserted, "You're only pretty as you feel." Today, PJ Harvey rants about women who try to look good for men only to have men sneer "you exhibitionist." Just on this one subject of appearance and self-image, it's easy to find three or three hundred sparks like these, songs or just lines that can provide access into a discussion or writing exercise about the subject, music acting as muse. We don't have to analyze the song—indeed, it's probably better not to, though occasionally it's useful to construct a coherent whole out of fragmentary lyrics. But getting the talk rolling on a potentially delicate subject is just one of many ways that music can be used as part of a process orientation, to provoke originality and stir up new life in tired writers.

This chapter details ways to use music to introduce some specific process steps and issues, but the value of the process orientation itself may be the most important message we can give to our students. As I discuss later, in Chapter 10, a huge percentage of our students are hobbled by romantic notions of the perfect first draft and of good writing as the natural, effortless product of inborn talent. If nothing else, a process orientation should help students understand the truth of the quotation that begins this chapter and believe in its application to writing.

Leads

"One, two, three, fawh," Paul McCartney counts off into the explosion that was the Beatles' first album. That absurdly simple opening can yield provocative insights into the value and importance of leads and of analysis.

There's no question that the success of a piece of either writing or music depends on its opening. Readers give the magazine article only a few seconds to interest them before they move on. But musical leads may be even more important. Hennion quotes "one head of a large international [music] firm":

> They really understood the trick back in the heyday of English pop music in the sixties: "The House of the Rising Sun," "Satisfaction," "A Whiter Shade of Pale," perhaps the biggest hits apart from those of the Beatles, all three made it on the strength of their introduction. You remember the guitar arpeggios of the Animals, the bass in "Satisfaction," the Hominid organ in "Whiter Shade of Pale." (190)

What hooks us? Can we make sense of what attracts readers and listeners and therefore learn how to create better leads?

When I was first pondering such questions and wondering if music could shed light on them, McCartney's famous opener popped into my mind for hopelessly idiosyncratic reasons. That count off of energy and delight no doubt affected other people, but the reason it hooked me on the Beatles seemed silly and unique to me.

I first heard the count in imitation. During sixth-grade winter gym class, the cool kids led by Pips Hopkins and Drew Shaw huddled in their corner apparently competing to count to four. Very odd. But because they were the cool kids (all of them destined to leave the school within the next two years, casualties of their coolness), I wanted to figure out what they were doing. Soon I was listening to Paul's original and imitating it myself. Then I bought Drew Shaw's old guitar and learned to play Beatles songs . . . .

As long as my story started (or stopped) with Pips Hopkins, it seemed pointless—although Pips was a popular guy for a while, I'm convinced Beatlemania would have happened without him. But when I asked myself what Pips was responding to, I began to see a different picture: those first seconds of not-yet-music capture the essence of what made the Beatles popular. The act of counting off the beat is probably almost as old as music itself, but the Beatles would have learned it from African American blues (or perhaps jazz) players. Their interest in and imitation of black blues and R&B was one of the pillars upon which their sound was founded, one of the reasons for their popularity. As Elvis Presley proved and everyone since has confirmed, white audiences have an insatiable hunger for black music filtered through white sensibilities. And that unique white Beatles sensibility was the other part of the magic—Paul's cute Liverpool accent, the sense of urgency and fun that characterized the Beatles' early period, when listeners who didn't know about black roots saw the Fab Four as Buddy Holly reborn in Liverpool.

After I've shown my students the world inside the grain of the Beatles' lead, I sometimes encourage students to jot down the name of another song that has a catchy lead. We analyze why we are taken by that particular opening, and then we fill the board with the characteristics of effective leads, discussing which ones are applicable to writing, moving naturally into activities with written leads. Among the scores of such activities, my favorites are variations on popularity contests, well analyzed. (For a full discussion, see Dethier 1999, 114.) I have students read ten or twenty leads—either from pieces in our reader that we haven't looked at yet or anonymous student leads that I gather from a batch of papers and print out for the class. Students choose their favorite, we tally votes, then we go through the winners, trying to determine what makes them work, building a list of qualities of good leads on the board. There's often surprising agreement about the best leads, and the discussion gives us a chance to talk about issues that appear in leads and affect the whole paper—What questions does the lead raise that the paper needs to answer? What promises does it make that the paper needs to keep? How does the lead establish voice, authority, perspective?

Rehearsals and Spontaneity

Luckily for me, the popularity of the Beatles seems to cross generational lines better than anything this side of Dr. Seuss, and the world's best-studied musical group can teach us a lot about creative processes as well as leads. A particularly debilitating process notion that young writers cling to is that great art should be spontaneous, that the most creative, interesting, original work is the opium dream variety, the flash of brilliance that you need to write down quickly, preferably on gold tablets. Writers lulled by this idea invest their energy into setting up the perfect creative situation—perfect setting, tools, atmosphere, drugs—and tend to scorn revision because it's not spontaneous, it tampers with the results of the original creative impulse. Instead, they wrack their brains (or destroy their brain cells) trying to come up with the genius idea, and then in desperation turn in what little they've produced as though it were a genius idea, without bothering to support, detail, or bring it to life. From a writing teacher's standpoint, the problems with this approach are legion—besides encouraging writers to resist revision, it tends to make them see any criticism or even questioning as a challenge to their very being, an insult to who they are. But the romance of this approach—and its lack of discipline and hard work—make it perennially popular.

The "spontaneity or bust" crowd can point to the Beatles' first album as proof of their position. The Beatles recorded ten of the fourteen songs on the album that changed the world in a single day, February 11, 1963, essentially live (Massey, 40; Hertsgaard, 31–32). Very little time for fourth takes, revision, or rehearsal. I've spent four or five hours of studio time recording a single simple children's song. How but with spontaneous creativity could the Beatles have produced a song an hour that day?

While I would not want to diminish the importance of that session and the astonishing amount of creative energy the five of them (including producer George Martin) expended, the session could just as easily stand as a symbol of "practice makes perfect." For this was not a band auditioning for its first gig or a bunch of musicians pulled off the street to create the next Monkees or Spice Girls. These were young men who had been playing together for six or seven years. They had played long hours in Hamburg, learning to project over the crowd noise under horrendous acoustical conditions and to relax their throats to keep their voices through the marathon gigs, becoming accustomed to one another's rhythms and harmonies. George Martin says, "They were intensely curious and very demanding, and they often wanted something that wasn't possible" (Massey, 38). Spontaneity is the happy end result of endless practice. To Martin's astonishment, when he and the engineers broke for lunch on that long day, the Beatles stayed in the studio rehearsing (Hertsgaard, 32). Students need to learn what the Beatles knew long before America had heard of them—what Robert Frost called "the pleasure of taking pains" (Ciardi, 13).

Creative Process at Work

To combat romantic notions about how writers work, our students need to see creative processes in action: writers' notebooks, early drafts, marginalia, and revisions prove that writers rehearse, revise, resee, even when they're "spontaneous." Jazz has left us the best and most accessible rough drafts, perhaps because engineers and archivists realized that even abortive musical forays by the likes of Charlie Parker, Miles Davis, and John Coltrane had value. So besides the successful take, we can listen to seven different false starts of Bird (Charlie Parker) and Diz (Dizzy Gillespie) playing "Leap Frog." The recent release of "official bootleg" albums has allowed us to see trial versions of songs by both Dylan and the Beatles. We can play, for instance, the first take of "A Hard Day's Night" and hear Paul sing "all through the night" at the end of the bridge, a phrase dropped by the time they recorded the final version of the song. What difference does the change make? Why might they have axed the phrase?

A small change in a song can be like a small change in a poem—it can have a radical effect on meaning, tone, and voice. Most students don't write poetry, and many are unsure about the changes they make in their own papers—the papers seem so long, the changes so minute and unsure. Although even the greatest writers can work only one word at a time, I think many students are hesitant to revise because they can't see any appreciable results when they do revise. But they can appreciate small changes in songs. Often the hook of a song, the memorable part that sticks in everyone's head and makes people go back for more, is only a few seconds long, yet imagine what the song would be without it. Students can supply their own examples of favorite song hooks and can speculate about the effects a small change—like leaving out the hook—would have.

Researching for Real

No step in the writing process is more crucial than finding an appropriate topic, especially when the assignment requires research. Students tend to view research writing as inherently impersonal and flock toward well-known subjects—nuclear power, eating disorders, the drinking age—even if they have no real interest in them. The concept "pick a subject that matters to you" seems simple, yet many students don't get it, perhaps because they've played so long the game of figuring out what the teacher wants.

To make this important concept stick, I explain a real research question and model a real research process that I pursued. I want them to see that research is often the most logical response to curiosity or confusion.

For years, I have played either of two Buffy Sainte-Marie songs when I want to talk about Native American issues—"My Country 'Tis of Thy People You're Dying" and "Now That the Buffalo's Gone." When I first started playing them in class, I wanted to give my classes the words, but there weren't scores of song lyric websites to rely on, and I couldn't decipher a phrase that appeared in both songs and sounded like "Kensoah Dam." I wanted to get the words right for my students. Besides, I wanted to know what was so important about that dam, what made Sainte-Marie insert it into two of the most powerful protest songs I know. I had a real research question, and I wanted answers.

So I went to the library, and after trying several different spellings I discovered that the Kinzua Dam was built in the early 1960s on the Allegheny River, flooding across the Pennsylvania state line into New York, taking 10,000 acres of the Seneca people's Allegheny Reservation and wiping out Cornplanter's Grant, at the time still occupied by two hundred and thirty-two descendants of Cornplanter, who had signed the Canandaigua Treaty of 1794, "the oldest active treaty in the United States" ("A Broken Promise"). The Federal government seized land that it said in the treaty it would "never claim" and that George Washington himself had promised the Senecas "the right to sell and the right of refusing to sell" ("John P. Saylor").

If I had been writing a paper, this straightforward answer to my question would have been just the beginning of my work. For now that I know the details, I find the dam to be the perfect symbol of relations between the United States government and the continent's pre-Columbian peoples: its story includes arrogant, paternalistic attitudes toward Native Americans, the willingness to break any promise to ensure the welfare of white citizens (or at least a pet project of the Army Corps of Engineers), and a refusal to grant Native American tribes the same rights as either Americans or foreign citizens.

I encourage students to look—perhaps into their own music collection—for such real research questions, questions they want answered for reasons other than to fulfill an assignment. Some need to look no further than the Sainte-Marie songs I played, which are packed with details worthy of investigation. One student wrote,

> I think the Buffy Sainte-Marie song you played inspired me to focus a lot of my writing on Native American issues because I was thinking about humanity a lot last term and her music is so emotional and direct—she really spoke to me about some issues historic and present that are not being dealt with. (Lester)

Collaboration

Writers collaborate almost as much as they revise, yet many students and teachers fear collaboration, partly because they have extreme and unrealistic ideas about what collaboration is. They picture three or four people sitting around a seminar table—or, worse yet, huddled around a keyboard—coming up with a phrase, deriding that into oblivion, trying under even more stress to find another phrase.

The reality is that people define collaboration in scores of different ways, and for some the benefits of collaboration can be achieved through phone conversations, e-mail, or letters. How the collaborators define the roles—or how the roles evolve as a result of personalities—has a lasting effect on how the participants work and feel about their work. So it's worth spending the transition time of class one day to expand their musical and process repertoire by playing "Take the A Train" and discussing Duke Ellington's collaboration with Billy Strayhorn. Strayhorn wrote some tunes (like "Take the 'A' Train") that Ellington played, but he was also often Ellington's arranger—he would take Ellington's melodies and score them for Ellington's orchestra. Martin Williams says of their collaboration, "perhaps we shall never know in detail who has contributed what to the Ellington book from the day Strayhorn joined him" (118). Maybe Ellington valued the same quality in Strayhorn that impressed Dizzy Gillespie: He did "the unexpected. Where everybody else goes this way, [he went] in the opposite direction" (quoted in Gitler, 69). I'm not sure what in the world of composition would be equivalent to that kind of collaboration—one person writing a topic sentence, and the other writing the rest of the paragraph? One perfecting the thesis, and the other writing ten pages of support? Getting a class involved in that question can help them see for themselves the many possibilities inherent in collaboration and perhaps start thinking about which might appeal to them.

Students who play or sing in any kind of band or chorus can make their own contributions to class discussions about collaboration. Any non-solo music is by definition collaborative, and both modern jazz and rock present a fascinating variety of takes on the central tension between individual and group. Cream generated excitement by having the bass and sometimes the drums pursue essentially individual lead melodies rather than simply provide a bottom for the lead guitar. In his last few years, John Coltrane made recordings that took this principle to an extreme that I don't yet understand, with a whole orchestra of soloists creating, it seems, their own melodies. Sleater-Kinney's collaboration puts a female spin on the kind of collective equality that made the Beatles so good; in songs like "Burn, Don't Freeze," singers Brownstein and Tucker pursue independent vocal (and guitar) lines that are closer to counterpoint than to harmony but that add up to more than the sum of the parts.

A number of scholars have explored various forms of collaboration and genre mixing that involve classical composers, poetry, and ballet. Teachers interested in such mixtures should consult Paul Oehler's discographies "American Literature Set to Music," Michael Hovland's *Musical Settings of American Poetry: A Bibliography*, Robert Spaethling's essay "Literature and Music," and Chapter 5 of Barrett, McCoy, and Veblen's *Sound Ways of Knowing*, "Exploring Relationships Among the Arts."

Active Reading, Writing, Listening

Lynne McNeill, who cotaught a graduate class with me and listened to my music each day just as the students did, called my attention to a particularly valuable lesson she'd learned about *active* processes.

> I realized how easy it is to let music happen to me, rather than interacting with it. When we would enter the room and you'd have a certain song on, it was easy to treat it just like the radio was on, to tap feet or fingers, to hum along if I knew it, without ever thinking about why you'd picked it or what you expected it to say to us or what I thought it was saying to me. When we all finally would lean forward and pay attention, so much more came out of the experience of listening. I think the same goes for reading. I love "letting books happen to me" sometimes, but that's not always the best way to get something out of them, especially books I'm reading for research purposes. Learning to apply the experience with music to reading, to finally grasp the difference between passive and active reading, is great. [Our] students need as many illustrations and examples as possible, and if they're not natural writers, finding those examples outside of the field of writing is, in my opinion, a huge benefit.

I have long struggled to find a good way to demonstrate to students the value of making their communicative processes more active—and there it was, right under my nose.

Expansion

Collaboration forces each student to take seriously the views and tastes of at least one other. Many students reflect back on collaborative projects saying they now see things in a different light; their tastes and opinions have broadened. This process of expanding a student's tastes, perspectives, and opinions is, I believe, central to most education. I try to model one kind of opening up by playing music that I initially didn't like and explaining how it grew on me. In Chapter 2, I discussed two ways my music appreciation has expanded—as a result of searching out the originals of cover versions I liked and of listening to students' and friends' enthusiasm and trying to hear what they're enthusiastic about. You can't see the effects of students' expanding tastes in any particular piece of their writing, but those tastes affect a student's whole approach to choosing topics and deciding how to focus them.

I play Marvin Gaye's "Let's Get It On" or PJ Harvey's "Dry" to discuss another way I've been motivated to expand—by reading. I started listening to PJ Harvey because I paid attention to a critic (the way taste is supposed to be spread). I read everything Gene Santoro writes in *The Nation*; I trust his taste. So I listened when he wrote an entire column on a single album—PJ Harvey's *Rid of Me*—and then two years later repeated the compliment when reviewing her third album. Santoro said things like "Harvey is resynthesizing—and in the process reimagining and redefining—the sound and shape of rock and roll" (715).

Because music, and particularly rock, is now as thoroughly infused in the atmosphere as particles of lead, we can get prompts about music from any number of cultural sources. When I play Marvin Gaye's "Let's Get It On" (which gets a chuckle from anyone who knows it), I talk about Nick Hornby's novel, *High Fidelity*, whose narrator, Rob, runs a record shop and amuses himself by constructing musical lists like the five best Elvis Costello songs. At what might be considered the climax of the book, the narrator reveals his five favorite songs—and at the top of the list is "Let's Get It On." By that point in the book, I believed enough in the narrator's (and the author's) musical taste that I took the suggestion seriously and listened more closely to a song that I considered, without thinking about it much, too overtly sexual or lascivious. And while it might not be on my top five, I now see why people are so enthusiastic about it, particularly the harmony on the second verse.

I encourage students to use similar prompts to expand their reading. Do they see the same magazine at the houses of two friends? Check it out! The novel that the character in the murder mystery is reading is probably worth a glance too. And most English majors are glad to provide lists of their favorite books. Students pick up clues to what's cool, what's worth paying attention to, from many sources. English teachers can help guide and expand students' "cool" lists by linking books and music and by demonstrating how often literature appears in pop culture.

Unplugged Revisions

MTV Unplugged and its imitators have done a significant favor for the listening public: they have made acoustic—or at least semi-acoustic—music fashionable again. Transforming electric, heavily engineered studio tracks for live acoustic broadcast requires significant revision and rethinking. These transformations reveal how talented people change their approach depending on the purpose, audience, and tools available to them. How does Eric Clapton take the quintessential electric guitar song, "Layla," and play it in the intimate, acoustic format of *Unplugged*? How does Arrested Development take the studio complexity of their music and simplify it so they can perform it live? Discussing such questions can help student writers understand how radically they may need to transform their message when writing for a different audience and purpose.

Music: Part of the Process?

Should we whistle while we work? Should music be part of our in-class writing process? Many writers, both students and professionals, report that listening to music makes writing more fun, easier, less onerous. "I've never willingly written a word without listening to music of some sort," says novelist Edmund White. "I wanted to keep writing until the music stopped" says undergraduate Cathy Larsen of an all-night paper-writing session accomplished with the help of the four unrepeated hours of piano music available on Jon Schmidt's website.

But playing a piece of music for a class of twenty-five or thirty students is a different matter. It would be unusual to find more than a handful of people in the same class inspired by the same music. Mahler might put the fire in student A's pen, Midler in student B's, Minor Threat in student C's. And certain music might destroy their concentration. I wouldn't want my students choosing musical selections for me to write by, and I'm sure they'd be equally skeptical of my choices. Playing music while asking students to work is an imposition; it *forces* music on the student, and I want music always to be an option.

On the other hand, my colleague and former student Matt Irwin plays music softly throughout class and finds that the vast majority of students enjoy the music. And because it tempers the awkward silence of an unanswered question, it helps Matt let the silence last longer. Increasing a teacher's "wait time" is such an important goal that Matt's experience makes me rethink my own resistance to "background music."

Feedback

If done well and received well, feedback can be a form of collaboration. But that's a big if. I tell my classes that the worst thing they can say about a peer's paper is "this sucks." But that's much rarer than the second-worst thing they can say: "This is fine." Avoiding these two extremes is the essence of good peer response, and examining the term *feedback* can help us understand how to provide such response.

As one of my students pointed out once during this discussion, the root of the word is *feed:* our comments must feed the author. Donald Murray says the key question about any response to a piece of writing is, Does it make me eager to get back to my writing desk? (2001a, 222). If it doesn't, then the feedback has failed.

But there's another side to feedback. When we talk about feedback in a writing class, we're of course borrowing the term from electronics. The term was first used in the 1920s to talk about problems in radio transmissions, but most students know it from its use to describe what happens when a microphone (or electric guitar) is too close to a speaker, and the sound from the speaker feeds back into the microphone in an endless loop that turns into an eardrum-piercing shriek. So electronic feedback has two salient features: it provides information, and it's annoying and painful.

People have probably been experimenting with feedback as long as there have been electric guitars, but it wasn't until the 1960s that guitarists like Jimi Hendrix tamed feedback enough to make it a standard part of the rock guitarist's repertoire. Kurt Cobain, one of the most innovative post-Hendrix guitarists, expanded the guitar's range of sounds, and rather than use them as ornamentation or distraction, he made them part of the edge and the attitude of the music. To open a discussion about feedback, therefore, I play "Radio Friendly Unit Shifter" from Nirvana's final studio album, *In Utero*. After some electronic madness at the very beginning, grating, high-pitched feedback shrieks follow, broken finally by a heavy drum-bass-guitar riff that feels like such a relief because the screeching is over and the music is progressing in a recognizable way—with a beat and a tune and sounds that more easily fit the definition of music. Yet the feedback makes the intro; you couldn't skip it and jump directly into the head-banging music with anywhere near the same effect. It's another successful experiment on the disputed border between noise and music.

For student critics, one implication of a detour into the history of feedback is that feedback almost always contains an unpleasant, grating component. If it's true feedback, it's impossible to make it entirely pleasant. Writing class feedback should be *feeding* the writer but also putting a burr in the writer's saddle or a nettle in the writer's socks.

I don't introduce the unpleasant side of feedback until fairly far into the semester. Initially, I don't want students thinking in evaluative terms at all; I want them to narrate the experience of reading the paper: "At first I thought your title referred to the school mascot, but then when you bring up Dobermans in the first paragraph, I decided you were really going to focus on dog shows, so then that detail about the umbrella threw me . . . ." I try to keep peer reviewers talking about what they know—their own feelings and thoughts as they read the paper—rather than stray into speculation, guesses, and judgment about what works or what should be done differently. But by the time I play "Radio Friendly," I want students to be pretty blunt about their reactions: "I get lost in . . . ."

Before the First Draft

This chapter's discussions of musical processes lead naturally into discussions of and experiments with writing processes. We can model writing collaboration, revision, and feedback on musical examples. Perhaps most important, we can borrow from music ideas about how to get started, what to do before the first draft. And those ideas inevitably lead writers to a better understanding of what we mean by writing process.

When I was in high school, before the process movement in composition began, we would write our papers, usually on assigned topics, turn them in, and get them back with a numerical grade and red marks indicating where we had transgressed. Somehow, magically, we were supposed to do a better job on the next paper. The red marks occasionally helped us avoid the same mistake the following week, but how we got to that grammar-checking step, how we would produce the drafts that we could then edit and proofread to catch the misspellings and passives, was a black box: the assignment would go in one side and a ready-for-proofing draft would miraculously appear out the other side.

But now we have thousands of articles and books to help us examine, analyze, and suggest alternatives for what goes on in that black box, and I think a writing teacher's greatest asset is a head full of suggestions for helping students over writing blocks and fears, approaches students can use to get something on paper and then organize, focus, and otherwise improve that initial outpouring. Numerous process activities approximate the kind of rehearsals that we can hear in the Charlie Parker outtakes; they produce the fragments and false starts that not only lead to the final take but may, as in Parker's case, be worth saving in their own right. Most use some variation of freewriting, the writer's greatest tool. As one of my ex-students put it, "I look forward to writing papers because it gives me an excuse to write freewrites, and I find myself writing freewrites about things I'm interested in and might want to write about later" (Larsen). Teachers interested in discussions of and explanations about process methods can consult almost any current writing textbook, but my favorite is still Donald Murray's *Write to Learn*.

Nine

Relating

*If we are indeed peninsulas rather than islands, music is often what
connects us to the mainland of humanity.*

*Perhaps this chapter should have come first, since helping people
relate in myriad ways, bridging gaps between people, is one of the
most basic functions of music and writing. This chapter will explore
ways to exploit this relational bridge in the classroom.*

"Hello in There"

John Prine's "Hello in There" is one of the most depressing songs I
know, yet it also highlights one of music's most important and successful themes and functions—creating a bridge between people. In
Prine's song, the age gap looms large, as the narrator and his wife fade

into their numbed minds and withering bodies. He paints a bleak picture of the end of life, and he makes it clear that the rest of us have a moral duty to try to reconnect, to say "hello in there."

Infatuation may be the most frequently articulated emotion in popular songs, but it certainly isn't the only one. Song lyrics offer every kind of relationship, every form of connecting, from the father-son bond of Kenny Loggins' "Danny's Song" to the Rolling Stones' "Sympathy for the Devil." Music is always on some level about relating; we sing at marches and rallies and funerals, any time disparate people try to meld into one. And though many musical messages—especially rock's—are about adolescent-macho posturing and competition, "musicians recognize also a responsibility to remind us of our vulnerability" (Dettmar 2000a, B9); songs can elicit feelings for others, produce empathy and, yes, as Dettmar says, make us cry.

After opening a class with something like Prine's plea for human connection, I turn to my students and ask, How has music helped you relate to people outside your normal social circle? Students may never have thought about it, but the singers they listen to and the characters in some of their favorite songs almost certainly come from racial and socioeconomic backgrounds different from theirs. Some students may listen to African, Jamaican, or South American music, but even those with the narrowest musical taste know something about life across the continent and across the Atlantic just from listening to pop hits. Students who have been in choirs have probably sung songs from other cultures, maybe in other languages; many choir directors these days try to reduce the Christian emphasis in Christmas concerts by sampling holiday music from a variety of faiths and cultures. Given a few examples and an invitation to talk about their favorite music, almost all students will be able to suggest ways that the music in their lives has helped them understand and appreciate different kinds of people.

Music and the "Other"

Now more than ever, English teachers need music's ability to connect different people, because concern for the Other—the person on the other side of the gap caused by poverty, race, orientation, age, gender, nationality—motivates much current humanist thought. For the past forty years, we have been gradually realizing that we should pay more attention to the Other, give the floor to traditionally excluded voices, value the contributions of overlooked groups, expose and battle the oppression that made them Other, see the connections that white male Americans have with women, African Americans, other racial minorities, other nationalities . . . and maybe someday we'll get to other socioeconomic classes.

A superb aid in helping us see such connections is Michael Ventura's essay, "Hear That Long Snake Moan." Ventura traces many of the defining characteristics of current rock music and rock concerts back through New Orleans and the Caribbean to West Africa, arguing that the attraction of African music for American audiences has always been that the culture from which it sprang rejected the Christian mind/body split, celebrating instead times when mind and body were one, as in a voodoo trance—or a fifteen-year-old pogo-dancing at a Phish concert. Teachers wanting to flesh out their general idea that the roots of American music go back to Africa, and perhaps hoping to broaden their students' attitudes about people to whom they can relate, would do well to invest a couple of hours in reading Ventura's article.

Reach Out: Music of the Sixties

Music has played a role in each wave of social transformation and awakening. And the songs associated with each transformation can play the same role on a smaller scale today, helping our students connect with others.

I'm a child of the 1960s, but I rejected the hippie label (I was more focused and less mellow than hippies were supposed to be) until people like Dr. Laura began to pin every social ill of the modern world on the counterculture insurgency of early baby boomers. As the national pastime of blaming the victim becomes ever more popular and the possibility of granting the Other respect, or at least a hearing, becomes more remote, the 1960s look better and better. Of course we need to remember the many blind spots of the 1960s counterculture and the distance between some rock musicians and the hippie movement. As rock critic Robert Palmer reminds us, "Pete Townshend threw Abbie Hoffman off the stage at Woodstock" (Obstfeld and Fitzgerald, 52).

Yet the central message of sixties rock about the Other was clear: "Get Together" (Youngbloods), "Reach Out of the Darkness" (Friend and Lover), "He Ain't Heavy, He's My Brother" (Hollies). Many political leaders, and much of the music of the time, was infamously misogynistic, but of course music heralded the changes in gender relations: think of Aretha Franklin (singing Otis Redding's song) demanding "RESPECT." Bob Dylan taught us when to be enraged about racist injustice ("Lonesome Death of Hattie Carroll"), and his alliances with folk, blues, country, and Christian music have prompted his fans to see more value in those other genres.

One of the great lessons about respect came from the blues. Our heroes—from the Beatles and the Stones to Janis Joplin and the Blues Brothers—worshipped black blues players of an earlier generation—Muddy Waters, Howlin' Wolf, Ray Charles—so we learned to say those names with reverence and accept that the masters were black. When Dylan turned electric—throwing an important Other in the face of folkie fans—he did it with a racially integrated blues band, Paul Butterfield's.

Of course while white rockers were reaching out, some black music was reflecting the new emphasis on black pride and community. Afrika Bambaataa of the Renegades of Funk says, "What got me excited first was when James Brown came out with 'Say It Loud—I'm Black and I'm Proud.' That's when we transcend from negro to black" (Toop, 58). Much of white America, egged on by the racist paranoia of "leaders" like FBI director J. Edgar Hoover, saw 1960s black militants like the Black Panthers as the greatest threat since the commies, but black performers like Otis Redding, Aretha Franklin, the Temptations, and Sly and the Family Stone managed both to promote black unity and to appeal to white audiences, giving some hope that if the revolution that Jefferson Airplane called for ever occurred, it would be an integrated one.

Popular music of the 1960s often fixated on the Other as a romantic hero. Songs like the Crystals' "He's a Rebel" glamorized the James Dean kind of Other. Big, bad John (Jimmy Dean) was kinda quiet and had a troubled past but he saved those miners. Janis Ian became famous at sixteen for singing about racial prejudice at the level of a high school date, the white girl's mother saying of her black date, "he's not our kind." The Beatles spoke for—or at least about—the Fool on the Hill and the Nowhere Man and poor lonely Eleanor Rigby. Like Patches (Lee), one of the tragic lovers of the period always lived on the wrong side of the tracks.

Christenson and Roberts note that "The politics of Woodstock . . . is giving way to what we call a 'politics of attitude'" (133). I wonder if the continuing popularity of sixties music results at least in part because some listeners are tired of modern "attitude" and want to return to "love is all."

Reach Farther: World Music and Bob Marley

First brought to American audiences by aging 1960s musicians like Jerry Garcia, Paul Simon, and Ry Cooder, world music today embodies some of the best hippie ideals. It's a marketplace of exchange where Bulgarian women's choirs mingle with Ladysmith Black Mombazo and throat singers from Tibet. Listening to the music of another culture is perhaps the fastest way to appreciate that culture, for open ears will almost always hear beauty in the very different languages and harmonies.

I don't think the term *world music* had been invented when Bob Marley started playing, but twenty years after his death, Marley is still the great musical ambassador, carrying to all points of the globe his Jamaican sound born of the worship of Ethiopian emperor Haile Selassie and of marijuana. Marley's music commands almost unanimous respect across all social and political boundaries; it is as close to universal as any cultural product can get. Marley mixed messages of pride, dignity, even revolution with assurances that we'll "feel all right" if we "get together." I imagine students are fascinated when a teacher makes Marley and his music the focus of a unit of study, as Alice Chumbley Lora did. Where did that rhythm, so easy on the world's ear, come from? Why did it meet resistance in white America? Do Marley's drugs and religion have anything to do with his music?

None of this of course brings to our stereos the Otherness of, say, a Vietnamese or Iraqi peasant dying of the Pentagon's great euphemism, *collateral damage*. The alienation in most rock songs is not that of class or nationality or religion; it's much closer to the almost universal alienation of adolescence, a time when many of us feel we don't fit in. We're all convinced we're Other. But because of that feeling, teenagers may be more likely to reach out to radically different people than would adults who are more comfortable with their place in society and therefore have less empathy for the alienated. We often mock the idealism of the young, but through songs about dreams and progress, music keeps alive the possibilities. For many people, music is the one thing that stands up to the dominant culture and asks, in the words of Nick Lowe, "(What's So Funny 'Bout) Peace, Love and Understanding?" (Costello).

Reach Across Generations

Even teachers who never play music in their classes can use music to relate to their students. In fact, long before I brought a boom box to my classes, music regularly reduced the distance between my students and me. Students would jot down their musical interests on their first-conference questionnaires, and when I glanced over their questionnaire I would say, "Hey, do you have Patti's latest one yet?" or "So which is your favorite Marley album?" or "Minutemen? Never heard of them. What do they do?" I've met very few students who aren't eager to talk about their musical choices.

Listening to the music of different generations playing together can help students overcome their sense that their music (or writing or dress or virtually anything else) is irreconcilably different from that of older generations. Violinist Stephane Grappelli (1908–1997), whose career spanned seven decades, is a useful figure for demonstrating that age alone doesn't have to create a generation gap. Grappelli first achieved fame playing with guitarist Django Reinhardt in Quintette de Hot Club de France in the 1930s. Reinhardt died in 1953, but Grappelli was playing well into his eighties. He recorded mostly with jazz musicians like Oscar Peterson (their version of "Them Their Eyes" is as good an introduction to jazz as I can think of), but perhaps his most accessible recordings were with folk/bluegrass/jazz mandolin player David Grisman, thirty-seven years his junior. Cuts like "Minor Swing" from Grisman's 1979 album *Hot Dawg* have almost universal appeal and demonstrate that in music—as in literature—art and ability cross all boundaries.

Breaching the Wall of Grades

The chorus of kids demanding to be left alone by their teachers in Pink Floyd's *The Wall* rightly haunts some of us. Of course I (mostly) reject the song's implication that teachers are out to do harm, but I think it's healthy for us to ask ourselves often whether we're doing something *to* our students, and why. And I find the metaphor of the wall particularly useful, especially since even in 2002 in a predominantly Mormon school, most of my students know Pink Floyd's 1979 hit.

So I play it on the day when I first hand out grades. I explain that I don't want grades to be a wall between us, and that I hope they will come talk to me rather than be aggrieved about a grade. "We've been building up a pretty good relationship," I say. "Let's not let the wall ruin it." And I keep playing music, hoping, as Keith Richards put it, that "eventually the music will cross that wall" (quoted in Obstfeld and Fitzgerald, 7).

Write in Another's Shoes

How can we build on the kind of intercultural, interpersonal bridges that I've discussed constructing with music? How can we get students to feel, believe in, and write about the kind of "one world" sentiments proclaimed by the song lyrics they listen to?

Perhaps the most successful writing assignment I've ever given, in terms of its effect on the writers themselves, was one of the simplest. In my first postgraduation job, I taught at a voc-tech college, three sections of College Writing and one of Interpersonal Communication, something in which I had no background. Luckily I had inherited a textbook to guide me. The class was, if I remember right, entirely male, young men learning to be auto mechanics. And our curriculum was as basic as it comes—learning to talk, communicate, get along. One day, I asked the class to think of a recent argument they'd had with a girlfriend (I gave them alternatives—parents, buddies—but I believe all wrote about girlfriends) and then write a page about the argument from the girlfriend's perspective.

I feared these guys with battery-acid holes in their denim jackets would revolt against the sappy, touchy-feely nature of the assignment; I certainly wasn't prepared for the response I got the next day. Many eyes were, literally, wider than they had been the day before; one tough mechanic after another said, "Wow, I never realized . . . ." I flattered myself that there were a couple dozen young women in the area for whom I had achieved hero status.

I haven't repeated that exact assignment—it fits better in an interpersonal communication course than in most English classes—but I do often use variations of an assignment popular in persuasion and argumentation books—writing from the opposite perspective. Some teachers take such an assignment to an extreme, asking students to take a stand on an issue and then write an entire paper from the opposite perspective. While that assignment can be useful for teaching argument and opening eyes, I get nervous about forcibly removing a writer's beliefs and opinions from the writing situation. So I feel more comfortable just asking that, somewhere in the process of writing a "taking a stand" paper, students spend five or ten minutes amassing arguments for the other side. Imaginatively putting themselves in another's shoes may help students develop more empathy for those on the other side, and it will almost certainly enable them to make their own paper stronger by predicting and undercutting the other side's best arguments.

A similar strategy can be used in literature courses: students can write from the perspective of marginalized characters. What do Widow Douglas and Miss Watson feel when Huck apparently dies? What does Jim think when Tom makes him the center of an absurd storybook rescue? What do the faithful black servants in Southern novels think of their employers? How did Dame van Winkle feel about Rip's long nap? What's going on in the female characters' heads in Hemingway's fiction? Spending time with Other characters and perspectives in music prepares students to make such imaginative leaps and therefore gain empathy and understanding for the characters, but unless asked specifically to do so, they sometimes won't make the leaps on their own.

Ten

Attitude Is Everything

A teacher who crosses the boundary into the lands of the teen-age electronic tribes might suddenly discover he is getting through to the hardest to reach in his class.
Jeffrey Schrank, English teacher, 1967

The title of this chapter exaggerates. After all, I also tell my students that voice is (almost) everything. But in a sense the title is accurate, because unless a writer has a good, or at least a functional, attitude, nothing else really matters—the writer won't produce anything. I work with students who have a wide range of debilitating attitudes— they hate school or they hate writing or they think they write fine and have nothing to learn or they think that writing springs full-blown from the writer's head.

Whether arising from despair or arrogance, these attitudes almost inevitably lead to procrastination that results in papers (and grades) not as good as they should be, and this failure tends to reinforce the bad attitudes and the procrastination, leading to a vicious downward spiral of attitude and output. I'm not arguing that there is a single best attitude or approach. My goal is to identify and expose attitudes that keep writers from doing their work and modify those attitudes with music.

It's Not the Subject, It's What You Bring to It

I write Name That Tune on the board and start playing John Coltrane's "My Favorite Things." Students who hear the beginning sometimes get it. Students who wander in later usually don't. Most know the song and smile when I say, "After hearing the Julie Andrews version a few times, I didn't think I ever needed to hear that song again." But when Coltrane plays it, it's fresh, exciting, and leaves me whistling. He taught me that the melody—the subject—matters less than the personality of the person playing it.

I spend much of the first week of a writing class trying to get young writers to believe that they have something of value to write about. Students sometimes think they need to have had unique, exotic experiences to write a good essay, and it may be difficult to persuade them that it's not the brilliant idea or the terrifying adventure that makes a great paper, it's the way the writer handles the material. They've probably heard that there's no such thing as a new subject, but they may not see that that fact liberates them from the futile search for a BIG IDEA. I want them to forget hunting for the unique and brilliant and instead find something that fascinates them. The best papers explore a fascination.

Students may not like Coltrane's version of "My Favorite Things" (or "Greensleeves" or "Chim Chim Cheree"), but my obvious reverence for the man gets their attention, and they understand the point that even the most tired, overplayed tune or idea can seem new, lively, and (to some ears) wonderful if a creative person approaches the old with fresh insight. I emphasize that while none of my students may be geniuses on a par with Coltrane, if they pick a subject that interests them, honestly and thoughtfully pose and try to answer questions that they really care about, and use specific details from their own experience and reading, they will put their own personal stamp on their writing and make fresh and original even a paper about something as thoroughly discussed as adolescent relationships.

Redirecting Bad Attitudes

Like anyone who teaches Freshman English, I get my share of students who don't want to be in school and most certainly don't want to be in English class. Angry at parents, teachers, authorities, or just life in general, they walk in the first day of class with a huge chip on their shoulders, ready to hate me and cause problems.

That attitude lasts until we meet for our first conference, when I express some interest in the music that the Angry Young Man (they are usually male, in my experience) professes to like. Such brazen attempts to bond with students succeed more often than the best flattery, perhaps because it would never occur to young men that someone would ask about their interest in Led Zeppelin or the Beastie Boys in order to draw them out. I've taught only one tough-guy student (who turned out to be a full-blooded sociopath) who didn't soften significantly after a short conversation about his favorite band. I'm certainly not claiming I can turn Tim McVeighs into model students; all I hope is that the student will decide I'm on his side and that together we can turn his angry energy into a spirited defense of Metallica or a scathing attack on political hypocrisy. It certainly helps that I can discuss the relative merits of X's first four albums—that I do have some legitimate interest and expertise on the subject—but even when I lack that, asking sincere questions and gratefully accepting the student's invitation to lend me the CD usually accomplishes the slight shift in attitude that I'm looking for.

. . . With Punk

Seth Kahn-Egan makes a compelling case for building a writing course around punk ideology. He identifies five "principles" of punk:

1. The Do-It-Yourself (DIY) ethic, which demands that we do our own work because anybody who would do our work for us is only trying to jerk us around;

2. A sense of anger and passion that finally drives a writer to say what's really on his or her mind;

3. A sense of destructiveness that calls for attacking institutions when those institutions are oppressive, or even dislikable;

4. A willingness to endure or even pursue pain to make oneself heard or noticed;

5. A pursuit of the "pleasure principle," a reveling in some kind of Nietzschean chasm. (100)

It's easy to see how these principles could worry society as a whole and potentially make teaching punk students a nightmare. On the other hand, that energy and outrage, if channeled and directed, can lead both to energetic writing and to the kind of questioning of institutions that can empower students and help them succeed in those institutions. As Kahn-Egan puts it,

> I'm advocating a classroom where students learn the passion, commitment, and energy that are available from and in writing; where they learn to be critical of themselves, their cultures, and their government—that is, of institutions in general; and, most importantly, where they learn to go beyond finding out what's wrong with the world and begin making it better. (100)

That's a tall order, and in his response to Kahn-Egan's article, Geoffrey Sirc questions the practicality and even the wisdom of an English class' trying to make the world a better place. But while punk is often thought of as negative and nihilistic, its principles *can* motivate and energize young writers. The do-it-yourself ethic puts the production of valuable art in reach of the average person—you don't have to sing like Judy Collins or play guitar like Jerry Garcia to make a great record. Sirc quotes writer Charles Young's 1977 meeting with Sex Pistols' singer Johnny Rotten (John Lydon), whom Young calls a "sickly dwarf": "if someone this powerless could cause that much uproar, maybe words still mean something" (1997, 22). In the worlds of both punk and rap, words have power. They're worth saying, and they may even change the world. Henry Rollins and Patti Smith and Ian MacKaye can scream about what irritates them and people will listen and buy the records and make them famous and they don't have to sell out or stop saying "fuck" or anything.

Punk arose partly as a reaction to the direction mainstream rock was going in the 1970s—becoming more professional, more technically adept, better produced, better marketed, and therefore necessarily more of a corporate product, not something the average person could create. Sirc sees a similar trend in composition—toward academic discourse, something that exists at least in part to assure a gap between the language haves and have-nots. If we truly want to make our students more conversant with academic discourse in order to empower them, rather than to make them slaves to that discourse, then a good dose of punk attitude might balance out more academic texts and tastes.

. . . With Rap

In the tide of recent writing about rap, a number of articles have argued for using rap to reinvent English classes. Geoffrey Sirc's "Never Mind the Sex Pistols, Where's 2Pac?" (1998) is a response to Kahn-Egan's article, quoted above. For those with some knowledge of gangsta rap, punk, and critical theory, Sirc's essay raises some central issues. Edward Anderson's "Rap Music in the Classroom?" is a much more basic starting point, as he defines rap, gives some of its history, emphasizes its positive messages, and lists five "ways to motivate and instruct students" with it (219). For those who want to understand the rap scene before they talk about it in class, David Toop's book provides an excellent introduction to the origins of hip-hop, and he mentions the attempts of people like Jimmy Castor (who in the late 1950s took over from Frankie Lymon as front man for the Teenagers) to use rap in the classroom.

> I figured that if you could at least motivate kids to be interested enough in reading that's the first step. . . . [Kids] don't really see anything around them that indicates that there is any need to read anything. . . . [They] had to understand that Michael Jackson didn't just walk into the studio and start singing the tune! "So they write those songs?" You get that kind of reaction. (Jimmy Castor quoted in Toop, 45)

. . . With Their Own Words

As an activity like the one at the end of this chapter often indicates, the single most common reason for the bad attitudes in English classes is that so many students feel bruised and battered by red marks on papers, never being called on to read papers aloud, and poor grades. So one of the simplest and most effective ways to change attitudes is to say directly to each student, "You did well."

When I'm reading the first batch of papers from a class, I copy down a good sentence or two from each paper, one that's particularly well phrased, or humorous, or pithy, or that brims with insight or wisdom. I type all these "gems" into the same file, print a copy for each student, and then spend most of a class period going over the list, with everyone sharing what they particularly like about each sentence. Students enjoy praising their classmates, and they derive endless pleasure from hearing people gush about something they wrote. This simple activity has changed more long-standing attitudes toward writing than anything else I have tried.

Enjoy Words

Building a course around a particular kind of music is a radical move—maybe too radical for most of us to undertake. But we can nudge student attitudes by taking the less drastic step I've been advocating—playing a single song and discussing it for a few minutes. One such discussion can give students a different perspective on why we write.

Some people can't stand the singing of Robert Smith, of the British "mope" or "Goth" rock band the Cure. They think he whines or he's too precious, or they find his made-up face annoying. But I play one of his songs—usually "Disintegration," off the album of the same name—almost every semester because I want to talk about the concept *word drunk*. Smith's eight-minute songs—hundreds of words and dozens of images cascading forth—help students quickly understand what I'm talking about.

Word drunk has negative connotations, of course—out of control, self-absorbed, out of touch. I wish I could find a term without those connotations that would still convey the same sense of awe and appreciation and wonder and inebriation with words. But the concept is too important to ignore for want of a perfect term.

It's too easy, in almost any writing class, to get lost in purpose and audience and organization and coherence and correctness and clarity and communication and connection and forget the fun of writing, the joy of letting the words roll out of the mouth or stream onto paper or screen. No doubt many of our current students identify that joy, that energy rush with rap, and in listening to or imitating their favorite rappers they appreciate the sensual value of words: words as color and sound and texture and shade, words that feel good and sound good and taste good, phrases with a rhythm that makes you want to stomp your feet or snap your fingers, sentences like a long rapids on the Allagash River flowing in the sun between banks of spruce and alder.

I don't know whether Robert Smith felt that way when he sang those words, but when I listen to him sing I get in that canoe and start bobbing with the current, and I feel it even more intensely when I sing the song myself. It's a sensation not easily identified, labeled, or articulated, yet most writers seem to experience it at some point in their lives. Students need permission to make that feeling a major goal, and they need support in experimenting with form and content to find what brings on the sense of "flow" that Mihaly Csikszentmihalyi finds central to pleasurable human experience.

Battling the Inner Critic

The major impediment to experiencing "flow" is our own internal critic, the voice of judgment that knows everything could be better. It's a voice that plagues even the best writers.

Bob Dylan's "Blind Willie McTell" routs small talk from the class. The instrumentation—Dylan on piano, Mark Knopfler on acoustic guitar—is spare, the production intimate, the singing riveting. The room quiets to hear Dylan compress the history of African America into six verses, as the centuries of suffering and endurance are distilled in the person of blues singer Blind Willie McTell (perhaps best known to most of the rock world as the composer of the Allman Brothers' signature song "Statesboro Blues"). The narrator has his own blues, in part because, as the chorus keeps reminding him, no one can sing the way McTell could.

The irony? No one has ever sung the blues with more conviction and immediacy than Dylan on that song. To me, it's a peak song in the career of the greatest songwriter the world has known. Yet Dylan kept it off the album it was intended for, *Infidels*, and the public didn't hear it until the release of the *Bootleg* CDs in 1991. He wasn't happy with something, though the comments he's made about the song don't clarify his displeasure.

I'm not sure it's possible to write without battling an internal critic or editor. Without the editor, most of our writing would be wordy schlock. But the editor—or the "Watcher at the Gate," as Gail Godwin calls it—is always greedy for attention, not satisfied to improve on a first sloppy effort but eager to butt in, right now—right as you're writing this word—and let you know that it's a lame word, a stupid word, so VERY trite, a word so bad that its presence on the screen should make you quit without saving and go to bed.

So we develop ways to trick the Watcher into taking a nap, giving us a break, coming back in a few days. (My most effective approach is repeating the mantra, "It's good enough for now.") For most people, silencing the Watcher takes vigilance and self-discipline, and the Watcher is seldom absent for long. My Watcher is difficult to shut up partly because I usually think it's right, no matter what games I use to talk myself into continuing to put words on the page. I can't completely shrug off the feeling that I am in fact the best, most objective, most realistic judge of my own writing, and if other people would stop being nice and get real, they'd agree with me.

So I play "Blind Willie McTell" and tell students about Dylan's decision to leave it off the album to let them know that even the best writers producing their best work aren't always satisfied and may in fact not see the value that is obvious to the rest of the world.

Dealing with Failure

While Dylan's uncertainty about some of his work seems unfounded, some rock stars' real, public failures can put student shortcomings into perspective.

"For What It's Worth," one of Stephen Stills' songs on the first Buffalo Springfield album, doesn't have the rage, the punch, the insight of many of Neil Young's political songs. Apparently a reaction to the police putdown of a mid-sixties L.A. street gathering, it's more an observation than a call to arms. But the success of the song—the group's first hit—and of Buffalo Springfield in general must have been particularly sweet, because Stephen Stills was a failure. He had a goal in life, he went for it, and he didn't get it.

His goal was to be a Monkee, one in a long and distinguished history of groups created by businesspeople rather than the musicians themselves. Columbia Pictures wanted to create and harness its own version of the Beatles, complete with their own TV show and songs written and played by professionals. So they auditioned hundreds of people for this boy band, and Stephen Stills tried out and didn't make the cut.

The temporary failure of a hugely successful person will not, of course, convince all student writers to be more optimistic about their writing, but it's a start, and it can lead to a discussion of our definitions of success and failure. I think we can, without being hypocritical, define success individually and apply it generously. If Steve Stills craved the kind of success that awaited the Monkees, he may still not be satisfied. But he may have found types of satisfaction that rearranged his definitions of success—satisfaction from being part of the coolest, most admired group of its era; satisfaction of working and singing with the same people for years; the knowledge that he could make it alone or with a variety of others.

Similarly, writing teachers need to celebrate successes of many kinds—improvements in attitude, in peripheral skills (like typing or Internet use), in creativity or procrastination or adaptability. We need to celebrate as often as possible: a successful use of a semicolon, a first paragraph written without trauma, a good experience with peer critique. Some students have been graded on an absolute scale, with the teacher's concept of perfection at the top and all student papers falling short. We need to build our students' confidence by starting with wherever they are (in reality, what choice do we have?) and moving them as far as possible on as many fronts as possible—whether it's organization, mechanics, creativity, or audience awareness—and cheering every step in the right direction. We can keep our high grading standards but still praise any positive movement.

Revision Attitudes

While Watcher-induced paralysis stems from our insecurities, self-defeating attitudes toward revision stem from many sources, including arrogance and romantic misconceptions about writing. Resistance to revision keeps many student writers from improving. If students have done well in previous courses by turning in hurried first drafts, they seldom want to change that habit—who would, if it really produced the best work they were capable of? Such resistance, born of laziness, can be compounded by a student's swallowing the notion that the first creative outpouring is the best. "Why should I change it?

That's what I felt at the time. Any changes now would be dishonest to that moment." (Note the implicit assumption that the words perfectly captured the feeling of the moment.) Some writers also face a less ideological, more practical problem: "I don't know what to change."

I've mentioned several examples of musical revisions useful for showing students how radical revision can and often should be: the two versions of "Gloria" (Chapter 1), "Crossroads" (Chapter 3), "I Want You" (Chapter 4), and "Soul Kitchen" (Chapter 6). Simply playing such revisions can affect student attitudes; as a grad student of mine put it, "Having you play the two versions of Bob Dylan's 'I Want You' made me finally understand what revision is about. I now resee my papers whenever I have time to do so" (Bencze).

In these days of multiple "mixes" of the same song, students may well have a sophisticated understanding of revision in the genres they're most interested in. What's the difference between the original and the dance mix? Which elements have changed, and which stay the same? And what did the artist have to let go of in order to allow for any substantial revision? Encouraging students to do the analysis and make the judgments might lead them to have a better understanding of what *revision* can mean and more commitment to trying comparable revision in their own papers. If your students' musical heroes revise and remix, why shouldn't they?

Music and Accountability

Although the majority of the suggestions in this book are intended to help English teachers move in progressive directions, to implement some of the insights of the past forty years, music also has much to offer the teacher overwhelmed and constricted by *accountability, the basics,* and testing mania. Some students may improve such things as their vocabulary, their understanding of poetics, and their ability to make verbal analogies only if given a chance to understand them through music.

Many of such testable improvements in specific skills and knowledge can occur only if there is an underlying change in the student's attitude. And that is probably music's greatest gift—it can change the attitude of almost any student. Christenson and Roberts assert, "The major difference between popular music and other media . . . lies in music's unique ability to influence mood and emotion—to produce an 'affective effect'" (46). For years, some teachers have played music to soothe an unruly class, help reduce distractions during writing periods, or get students psyched for a test or an activity. Some students come to class primarily, it seems, to hear the music of the day, and sometimes the enthusiasm generated by hearing a good tune will carry students through the class period. Music wakes students up, helps them understand concepts and terms, enables them to see the relevance of the class subject matter. As Grossberg says, "the rock and roll culture transforms many of the structures of contemporary boredom (repetition and noise) into the structures and pleasures of its musical and listening practices" (1990, 116).

Write: The Best of Times and the Worst

If we want to change their attitudes about English, we need to get students talking about the origins of those attitudes. We can use songs like "Another Brick in the Wall" (see Chapter 9) or "Cemetry Gates" (see Chapter 3) to provoke such discussions.

By dealing openly with attitude problems, making them a legitimate topic of classroom conversation, we can at least let students know that we think attitude's an important subject, that attitude problems aren't just "all in your head" feelings students should get over, nor are students lame or weird for having them. If students can start by trusting us, connecting with us about something, maybe the attitudes themselves can change. An easy way into such discussion is to have students write about the best and worst experiences they've had in English classes.

The best experiences tend to be moments of recognition by teachers, peers, or occasionally award committees—while the worst are almost always comments by teachers that make us cringe. For instance, my student discovered in the textbook margin graffiti of a hexagon with STOP written in it. As she was supposed to do, she showed the doodle to her teacher, insisting, "I didn't write it." The teacher glanced at it and said, "I know you didn't. It's spelled right."

Asking students to unearth and discuss such moments can be embarrassing for us, but it serves several useful functions. It allows students to air and perhaps transcend the incidents in their past that produced bad sentiments. It allows teachers to align themselves with the aggrieved students and against the perceived cruelty of the past, a first step in helping students see that the Traumas of English Past don't need to be reenacted. It helps students realize that almost everyone has, sometime in their life, been singled out for imperfect writing, and therefore it raises the possibility that they might not really be such bad writers after all. And it opens lines of communication that students might use to report slights or misunderstandings in our own classes and get them resolved before they become more bad feelings. In McNamee's terms, it helps us "avoid abstract positions"; it puts into concrete terms the sense of fear and angst that many student writers feel about writing and allows us to be equally specific in addressing their concerns. To change student attitudes in the present, we may have to confront the historical sources of those attitudes.

Coda

When the end is in sight for what I'm swearing will be this book's final edit (before the FINAL final edit, when I cut out all the song quotations publishers won't let me use), I try for the first time the new technology in the classroom where I'm teaching American Nature Writers. Electronic components hide in a locked cabinet, speakers and projector hang from the ceiling, and a little black volume knob sprouts from the tabletop console. The classroom of the future.

At 12:28, I insert *Trout Mask Replica* into the fancy multidisk player. The awkward blats of Captain Beefheart's saxophone blast a bit too loud at first, and my hand jerks to the volume knob. The narrator of "Wild Life" is going to take his wife to a mountain cave and beg the bears to let them in.

I'm preparing students to discuss Jared Diamond's "The Worst Mistake in the History of the Human Race," his outrageous but convincing argument that agriculture has been a cursed experiment for the human species. Diamond's writing often seems ahead of his time, but Captain Beefheart beat him by twenty years in extolling the virtues of the hunter-gatherer life. Maybe the desire to escape into the hills is left over from 10,000 years ago, when a good cave was a palace.

The song reminds the class of "Wild Nights," the ecstatic Emily Dickinson poem we read six weeks ago. And it's another piece of evidence in an argument I hadn't intended to develop, establishing 1969–1970 as the year of the eco-song. Besides "Wild Life" and "Ant Man Bee" on *Trout Mask Replica*, think of The Beatles' "Because," Quicksilver's "Fresh Air" and "What About Me," Spirit's "Nature's Way," Neil Young's "After the Gold Rush" . . . the evidence seems overwhelming, and besides, it was the year of the first Earth Day.

But it was also my senior year in high school, a time of perhaps maximum susceptibility to musical influences, so I have to admit to perceptual bias, my interpretation inevitably swayed by influences of time and place.

I take thirty seconds to rant about *Trout Mask Replica*, arguably the greatest and possibly the strangest rock album that none of my students has heard of. I make a quick plug for expanding one's tastes, even into things that seem, at first, nothing but strange. I display the trout mask—actually a carp mask, I think—on the album cover.

It's 12:35, I've introduced one part of today's discussion, connected to previous texts and threads in the course, constructed and deconstructed a theory about the evolution of a major American movement, shed a little more light on the concept of social construction, and prodded students to move beyond the comfortable and familiar.

And with the sound of Beefheart's warbling sax echoing in my head, I start the class grinning.

Appendix A

God with a Big 'G'

Doug Smeath

Tori Amos' beliefs could be classified under 'C' for controversial. Instead, they are found under 'A,' for Amos, of course, in your nearby music store. There you will find any number of albums filled with lyrics that question God's right to act so tough. Albums suggesting that "feeling the word" is more possible through masturbation than meditation. Controversy, if you're into understatement. Yes, Tori has been called sacrilegious, ungodly, profane . . . Even the antichrist. But I am convinced that, were it not for Tori Amos' blessed blasphemy, I would not be a very spiritual person today. Chances are, I would instead be a very Mormon person.

My first discovery of Tori's music came at just the right moment in my life. I was at a friend's house in ninth grade. Religiously, I was a teeter-totter. "I could have gone either way." Either way. There's a quote I stole from my mom. To her, there are two ways: the right way and the wrong way, the way to salvation and the way to eternal damnation. And she loved to remind me of which way I was expected to go. But at times I was an avid believer, at other times an adamant skeptic. I wanted so badly for something to believe in that I was beginning to convince myself. I almost started to believe that I needed church, I liked church, I depended on church. I convinced myself that that excited feeling I got as I walked to seminary class was the Holy Spirit bearing Divine Witness, not excitement at the prospect of gazing at my Attractive Teacher.

At the same time, however, I was also freeing my mind. I was discovering how exciting it is to think for yourself. I admit—I was even taken by those so-called "Gothics." That's how in need I was of individuality—to me, their black clothes and black hair and face makeup—even for the boys—was the epitome of Holy Selfdom. Soon I realized that they were just conforming in a different way. So I kept looking for the Path to Personal Truth. While outwardly I marched onward with the Christian Soldiers, inside I was doing the nasty with that proverbial different drummer.

Enter Tori Amos.

We return to my friend's house where we see four ninth graders—
one of them me—recording a radio play one of my friends had written. The selected introduction music is a series of piano chords,
arranged just so, creating the kind of music that runs through your
head for weeks but never once annoys. The kind of music that
changes lives. The music fades once a woman's voice begins singing,
"From in the shadows she calls . . . ." Fades, and I am supposed to
enter with my first line. But I can't record. I ask who the musician is
and then demand to hear more of this song, this "Girl" by Tori Amos.

So they play it for me. They stop the tape and start the CD.
Hauntingly, backed by a drumbeat, the music creates an image. "And
in the shadow she crawls, clutching a faded photograph. My image
under her thumb, yes, with a message for my heart. [And now the
clincher.] She's been everybody else's girl. Maybe one day she'll be her
own" (*Little Earthquakes*). It was not a new concept to me, but no one
had ever sung it so beautifully or put it so clearly. I was everybody
else's girl. And I wanted to be my own.

So it begins. The next Sunday my friends have brought more Tori
music. They giggle as they tell me to listen to "this one." It's Tori's second album, they say. It's called *Under the Pink*, and this song, "Icicle,"
is about . . . Well, you'll figure out what it's about, they say. And Tori
sings. "Icicle, icicle, where are you going? . . . Will you keep watch for
me? I hear them calling. Gonna lay down . . . Greeting the monster in
our Easter dresses. Father says bow your head, like the Good Book
says. Well I think the Good Book is missing some pages . . . And when
my hand touches myself, I can finally rest my head." Wait—did she
just say . . . ? "And when they say, 'Take of His Body,' I think I'll take
from mine instead. Getting off, getting off, while they're all down-
stairs, singing prayers, sing away . . . Lay your book on my chest. Feel
the word. Feel the word." Yes! This chick was on to something! Okay,
sure, she was singing about masturbating. But she was singing about
escaping! About being your own release. No one had told me, ever,
that I could find peace, could find joy, on my own, with or without
God and the God Crew. So as my friends laughed at the physical
aspect of this song, they didn't notice that I was already being affected by the spiritual nature of it.

This is what Tori has always been to me. My friends love her, but
with great caution. She's too weird, they say, to take too seriously.
Even those who call Tori their favorite musician sometimes try not to
understand her. Too afraid of receiving the wrong kind of enlighten-
ment, maybe, they call her beautiful, call her talented, call her amazing. They stand in awe when they see her perform live. But then she
talks about masturbating, or being crucified. She calls Lucifer her

father ("Father Lucifer") or sees "everywhere a Judas, as far as you can see" ("Professional Widow"). And that's where my friends turn off. But that's just where I get started.

I still tried to cling to some sense of religion. Tori would make a great Mormon, I told myself. "I think the Good Book is missing some pages," she'd said. What good Mormon hasn't learned to argue apparent contradictions between the Book of Mormon and the Bible with this logic? "The Bible wasn't completely translated correctly," we'd say. "Missing some pages." So I clung. But, slowly, I was losing my grip . . . .

To say Tori Amos became my new scripture, my new prophet, my new savior would be inaccurate. I would learn with time that Tori, the daughter of a Methodist minister, included Muhammad, Jupiter, Jesus, Robert Plant, Buddha, and the faeries, among others, in her personal belief system. And she picked mercilessly on each of these, her inspirations. "Hey, Jupiter," she sings, contemplating the end of relationships, stability, sanity. "Nothing's been the same, so are you gay?" ("Hey Jupiter"). In "Muhammad My Friend," she tells Muhammad, "It's time to tell the world. We both know it was a girl back in Bethlehem." When she dies, she plans to be a "Happy Phantom," chasing nuns around and scaring them to death. No, to adopt Tori's mythology would be counter-productive. It would be the ultimate sacrilege. Tori's belief system is, to say the least, eclectic. To simply go along with everything she says just because she said it would be as bad as going along with everything your run-of-the-mill clergyman said. (Maybe even worse, because, to be honest, some of Tori's beliefs are, well . . . they're weird. Yes, I said it.) In *Little Earthquakes'* "Crucify," Tori sings about "looking for a savior in these dirty streets; looking for a savior beneath these dirty sheets." Six years later, in *from the choirgirl hotel*, she has found a new goal, a superior goal: "6:58, are you sure where my spark is? Here. Here. Here" ("Spark"). Don't look for saviors anywhere else until you have found your own spark of truth within yourself. Tori wants us to be our own girls. Not everybody else's. Not even Tori's.

So I took Tori's advice and stopped crucifying myself. I started looking for my own truth. And I found it. Or I found hints of it here and there by questioning and thinking and feeling and looking a little more deeply. Suddenly, long-standing assumptions—assumptions that had for so long ruled my life—came crashing down around me.

"Don't hide your light," they told me in church. "Don't hide who you are. Be yourself. Don't lie." But the Tori warning lights came on. This is a lovely little philosophy the church has here, but it's okay to question it, to question the church's intentions behind it. Why, if I should take what God gave me and run with it, should I keep hiding myself? Why should I deny my feelings of homosexuality and force myself to lie to those I love? Is that the exception to the rule? The church tries to tell me to be myself, to realize that I am a "child of God," but the "howevers" and the "on the other hands" are just too many to ignore. Tori's take on it is altogether more feasible—be yourself by finding yourself (if that's not too cliché), by basking by your own fire. The church says to be yourself on God's terms; Tori says to be yourself on your terms. Growing up gay, as I am sure everyone has heard by now, is a painful thing. It's lonely; it's empty. It's hopeless. Especially growing up gay and Mormon. Suddenly Tori was telling me to stop being a victim and start being myself.

Or the church would say, "God has a wife. We don't hear much about her because He respects her too much. He doesn't want her name 'abused,' as His is." Okay, that's an interestingly odd story. Or is the real reason what He says in Proverbs 31:3? "Give not thy strength unto women, nor thy ways unto that which destroyeth kings." Tori saw right through that one. "God, sometimes you just don't come through. Do you need a woman to look after you? . . . Will you even tell her if you decide to make the sky fall?" ("God"). To question the patriarchy that had always ruled my life was business risky enough. But to question the very founder, perpetrator, and perpetuator of that patriarchy—the Hebrew God, Elohim, the Great Jehovah Himself—was a dangerous relief—a relief well worth the sacrifice. Perhaps the only thing harder than being a gay Mormon is being a feminist male Mormon. Tori, who has been mistakenly taken for a militant "femi-Nazi," just wants honesty. The power of the female, the power of the feminist, is a power that has changed the world, and thank goddess for it! And the oppressive patriarchy we all know and love so well has been anything but honest about that. "Boy so hard, but I know a girl twice as hard," Tori sings ("Twinkle"). Girls are no better than men are, boys no better than women. All are vicious; all are venomous. Virtuous. Alone. In love. Human.

But if you disagree with Tori, don't argue with her unless you're prepared. She knows her stuff. (Yet another important religious rule I have learned from her—learn the facts first, then form your beliefs second.) She has no belief that she hasn't studied in depth. She knows the inside and out of the Celtic Fae. When she sings "the Lord of the Flies was diagnosed as sound" she knows enough to be using Satan's nickname from some long-forgotten myth or story, not just referring to that well-known book title ("Pandora's Aquarium"). She is fluently familiar with Persephone, "all the wizards black and white," Pandora, and Jesus. And then she puts it all together.

One thing I have learned from Tori is that truth is just the first step. I hear Tori acknowledge things that you'd at first never expect her to accept. Like the Christian variation of angels. In one interview, she talks about a story her mother told her. Two kids survived a hurricane and said they heard voices—angels—who saved them. Anyone who would expect Tori's reply to be, "Angels?! Get a life!" or even a slightly less cruel response, needs to think again. Tori actually says she believes the angels did visit those kids. But she won't settle on that— believing the angels came isn't a complete belief. Even if angels exist, Tori won't fall to her knees and cross herself. She'll make them pay; she'll expect some answers, quick. "But what happens when the angels don't come?" Now she's talking about the time God, the angels, the cosmos, and her own uterus betrayed her and let her miscarry (BoxTalk with Tori Amos, THE BOX TV Network). I myself have experienced missing an angel or two when I really needed them. When I knelt by my bed, begging for answers to all my religious questions. When I sat alone, an eight-year-old babysitting a neighbor's infant, at one in the morning, praying for some comfort, for an angel to hold my hand, or for my neighbor to just come home already. "Where are those angels when you need 'em?" ("Crucify"). Forming a belief is hard enough, but it's not enough. In the song "Spark," she sings, "If the divine master plan is perfection"—is Tori faltering, letting herself believe in Christianity? "maybe next I'll give Judas a try." There it is, the "but." So you can believe something is true. That doesn't give anyone the right to tell you what to do with that truth. No one but you can tell you where to stick it.

Before we get too far for what I'm about to say to even sound plausible, I have to clarify something. I love Jesus. I am eternally grateful to God. Or whoever it is that's in charge of all this. I am, really. But I'm not going to let Him, or Her, or anyone else, tell me whom to love, what to think, how to dance, what to smoke, where to go, when to cry, what to hear, or why to be. That's what Tori taught me. Just like in any other relationship, love doesn't mean abandoning your duty to self. ("So you can make me cum," she sings to "those Christian boys" in the song "Precious Things." "That doesn't make you Jesus.") That's what a personal relationship with God and Spirituality is about. Tori herself loves Jesus. "I used to think I'd make a great girlfriend for Jesus," she once said.

Tori's relationship with the deities, the myths, the prophets, and the monsters is the epitome of Tori's life. It's the basis. The only truth out there—the only cornerstone on which to base your life—is a personal relationship with your own spirituality. The power in Tori's musical spirituality is that it is not blatantly spiritual—it is pervasively spiritual. All of it, every aspect, every word prods the listener to open up gates inside him or herself. Once these gates start to open, they can't stop, and you realize that this is the way to go—that, in order to find an ultimate power and to use it in any form and for any purpose, you have to be willing to personally connect to that power. Tori forms a relationship with God that allows her to call him the "ice cream assassin" in the song "Spark," in the same familiar way a kid would tell his mom, "You always kill my fun." In "Father Lucifer," the relationship is with Lucifer, or more specifically, her own dark side, and she dances with it and learns to appreciate the dark parts of her nature.

Essentially, the eternal battle is religion versus spirit. For so long, I gave up my life to God, Sunday School–style. Now, Tori's taught me to be my own girl. Or boy. Just be my own. To go "Past the Mission" and smell the roses. To scream in cathedrals, and let it be beautiful ("iieee"). To not sacrifice letting it be beautiful, even if it means God has to plug His Ears. The ultimate God, the only one that really deserves a capital 'G,' is Self. Even God has to answer to HimSelf.

So, given the choice of going onward—and onward—and onward—with those tedious Christian Soldiers or staying back with the beat of that delicious different drummer, I now know whom to choose, thanks to Tori Amos. As she sings in "Beulah Land," "Give me religion and a lobotomy."

Appendix B

The Green Pillows

Kate Snyder

My family owns a pair of green corduroy pillows. We call them The Green Pillows. Capital letters for a proper name. The Green Pillows are practically family, maybe better. We have had them since I was a Glenwood Elementary School Gator, so they have gradually evolved into flat, pointed rectangles. However, by shaking all the stuffing into the wider part of the triangle, I can create a really solid head pillow. The corduroy has worn down a little, but it still leaves stripes on my face if I nap too long. Periodically, my dad declares that it is time for The Green Pillows to go, usually when a seam bursts. My brother Travis and I then quickly and passionately come to the rescue of The Green Pillows and defend their place in our home. Our rhetoric succeeds every time and my dad grudgingly gets his sewing kit and mends the damage. Ultimately, I think we all understand our family's need for The Green Pillows' reassuring predictability in a home that has become less certain.

Originally The Green Pillows belonged in my dad's UNC office which also housed some orange pillows of the same design. These pillows helped increase the comfort and homeyness of the office, which also belonged to Rob Chamberlain, an English graduate student like my dad. Eventually The Green Pillows ended up in our Chapel Hill apartment on Maxwell Road and have stayed with us through several moves.

These funky 70s pillows have no logical place in my family's house, which is filled with antique furniture, old quilts, and books. However, the house would not be home without them. We use these pillows. When my family watches a video together, we have designated locations. My mom lies on the couch and my dad sits on the floor next to her. My brother takes the futon. I lie on the floor with a Green Pillow fluffed just right or, if I'm lucky, both pillows stacked to form a square beneath my head.

When someone listens to music with headphones, they use a Green Pillow. As a child, one of my favorite activities was listening to records on my dad's big headphones, which covered most of my head.

After I was granted permission to use the stereo, my dad would fluff a Green Pillow, put the headphones on me, and cue the record. This father-daughter ritual substituted for the hugs and "I love you"s that my dad is reluctant to give. Sometimes I would listen to my own record collection, which included soundtracks from my favorite television programs, *The Muppet Show* and *Sesame Street*. Or I would choose one of my dad's records, the foundation of my love for rock music. While listening, I examined the cover and followed the lyrics. The Beatles' *Sergeant Pepper's* was one of my favorites. I never tired of looking at the cover: The Beatles in various eras including their colorful Sergeant Pepper uniforms, Marilyn Monroe, W. C. Fields. Yes, Bruce Springsteen, and Alan Parsons were also favorites.

Unfortunately, The Green Pillows, like other family members, have a dark side. Despite the pillows becoming gradually less stuffed, they can still be used as dangerous weapons. A pillow's impact can stamp a shocked expression on the victim's face that remains minutes after the pillow has dropped to the floor. Therefore, The Green Pillows have been banned from all pillow fights. Not to have the pillow's power completely stripped from him, Travis devised the "It's Raining Pillows" game. This game usually takes place while I or another victim is preoccupied with watching TV or talking to someone else. Travis then launches a Green Pillow up in the air and announces, "It's raining pillows!" By the time his statement sinks in, the pillow has hit the victim (usually me) right on the head. Travis will not say how he came up with this game, but does readily admit to longing for a vaulted ceiling which could allow more strategic pillow tosses.

Even with their dark side, I love The Green Pillows. They are a constant. They remain an essential part of my family's home despite moves, despite avocado green's going in and out of fashion, even despite changes in the family. My mom died while I was lying on a green pillow watching *French Kiss*. Two days after the funeral, my dad tried to throw the pillows away and Travis and I rallied on their behalf. It is a comfort to know that some things will not change.

References

Print

"Agreement on Guidelines for Classroom Copying in Not-For-Profit Educational Institutions with Respect to Books and Periodicals." 1976. Reproduced in Circular 21, available from the U.S. Copyright Office, http://www.loc.gov/copyright.

Anderson, Edward. 1993. "Rap Music in the Classroom?" *Teaching English in the Two Year College* 21 (October): 214–21.

Angelo, Thomas A., and K. Patricia Cross. 1993. *Classroom Assessment Techniques*. 2d ed. San Francisco: Jossey-Bass.

Baldwin, James. 1948/1994. "Sonny's Blues." In *The Heath Anthology of American Literature* vol. 2, edited by Paul Lauter. Lexington: Heath.

Ballenger, Bruce. 1999. *Beyond Note Cards*. Portsmouth, NH: Boynton/Cook.

———. 1990. "The Importance of Writing Badly." *Christian Science Monitor*, 28 March, 18.

Barrett, Janet R., Claire W. McCoy, and Kari K. Veblen. 1997. *Sound Ways of Knowing: Music in the Interdisciplinary Curriculum*. New York: Schirmer Books.

Barricelli, Jean-Pierre, Joseph Gibaldi, and Estella Lauter. 1990. *Teaching Literature and Other Arts*. New York: Modern Language Association.

Barry, Dave. 1997. *Dave Barry's Book of Bad Songs*. Kansas City: Andrews McMeel.

Bauldie, John. 1991. Liner notes to *Bob Dylan: Bootleg Series, Vols. 1–3*. Sony.

Bencze, Iren. 2002. Personal e-mail to the author. 15 January.

Black, Mary Ann. "British Romantics, Sixties Lyrics." In "Words and Music in the English Classroom." *English Journal* 80 (8): 81–82.

Blundell, Valda, John Shepherd, and Ian Taylor, eds. 1993. *Relocating Cultural Studies: Developments in Theory and Research*. New York: Routledge.

"Broken Promise, A." Accessed 12/19/01 at: www.carnegiemuseums.org /cmnh/exhibits/north-south-east-west/iroquois/kinzua_dam.html.

Capote, Truman. 1965. *In Cold Blood*. New York: Vintage.

Carter, Steven. 1969. "The Beatles and Freshman English." *CCC* 20 (3): 228–32.

Christenson, Peter G., and Donald F. Roberts. 1998. *It's Not Only Rock & Roll*. Cresskill, NJ: Hampton Press.

Ciardi, John. 1989. *Ciardi Himself: Fifteen Essays in the Reading, Writing, and Teaching of Poetry*. Fayetteville: University of Arkansas.

Coupland, Douglas. 1991. *Generation X*. New York: St. Martins.

Cox, Beth. 1991. "Comma, Comma." In "Words and Music in the English Classroom." *English Journal* 80 (8): 77.

Crafts, Susan D., Daniel Cavicchi, and Charles Keil. 1993. *My Music*. Hanover, NH: Wesleyan University Press.

Croft, Aaron. 2001. Personal e-mail to the author. 11 November.

Csikszentmihalyi, Mihaly. 1997. *Finding Flow: The Psychology of Engagement with Everyday Life*. New York: Basic Books.

Cvetkovich, Ann, and Gretchen Phillips. 2000. "Revenge of the Girl Bands." *The Nation* 271 (2): 16–17.

DeCurtis, Anthony. 1998. *Rocking My Life Away*. Durham, NC: Duke University Press.

Dethier, Brock. 1999. *The Composition Instructor's Survival Guide*. Portsmouth, NH: Boynton/Cook.

———. 1991. "Using Music as a Second Language." *English Journal* 80 (8): 72–76.

Dettmar, Kevin J. H. 2000a. "Don't Forget the Songs That Made You Cry." *The Chronicle of Higher Education* (7 April): B8–B9.

———. 2000b. "'High Fidelity': The Use and Misuse of Music for Life." *The Chronicle of Higher Education* (21 April): B11–B12.

———. 2000c. "Ironic Literacy: Grasping the Dark Images of Rock." *The Chronicle of Higher Education* (2 June): B11–B12.

Diamond, Jared. 1987. "The Worst Mistake in the History of the Human Race." *Discover* (May): 64–66.

Dickinson, Emily. 1960. "Tell all the truth but tell it slant" (1129) and "Wild Nights" (249). *The Complete Poems of Emily Dickinson,* ed. Thomas H. Johnson. Boston: Little, Brown.

DiPrince, Dawn, et al. 1994. *Row, Row, Row Your Class: Using Music as a Springboard for Writing, Exploration, and Learning*. Fort Collins, CO: Cottonwood.

Donne, John. [1624] 1952. "XVII Meditation. Devotions Upon Emergent Occasions." *The Complete Poetry and Selected Prose of John Donne*, 441. New York: Random House.

Durbin, Karen. 1974. "Can a Feminist Love the World's Greatest Rock and Roll Band?" *Ms.* 3(4): 23–26.

Emig, Janet. 1983. *The Web of Meaning: Essays on Writing, Teaching, Learning, and Thinking*. Portsmouth, NH: Boynton/Cook.

Erdrich, Louise. 1993. *Love Medicine*. New and expanded version. New York: HarperPerennial.

Erlewine, Michael, et al. 1997. *All Music Guide to Rock*. San Francisco: Miller Freeman.

Faulkner, William. 1936. *Absalom, Absalom!* New York: Random House.

———. 1930. *As I Lay Dying*. New York: Random House.

———. 1929. *The Sound and the Fury*. New York: Random House.

Fay, Marion. 2001. "Music in the Classroom: An Alternative Approach to Teaching Literature." *Teaching English in the Two-Year College* 28(4): 372–78.

Finn, Geraldine. 1993. "Why Are There No Great Women Postmodernists?" In *Relocating Cultural Studies: Developments in Theory and Research*, edited by Valda Blundell, John Shepherd, Ian Taylor. New York: Routledge.

Flanagan, Bill. 1994. "Frontman: John Lydon." *Musician* (July): 7.

———. 1986. *Written in My Soul*. Chicago: Contemporary.

"Forget the message; just play." 1967. *Time* 90 (17): 53.

Freire, Paulo. 1970. *Pedagogy of the Oppressed*. New York: Herder.

Frith, Simon. 1995. "Quote Unquote." *Popular Music* 14 (2): 257–60.

———. 1987. "Towards an Aesthetic of Popular Music." In *Music and Society*, edited by Richard Leppert and Susan McClary. New York: Cambridge University Press.

Frith, Simon, and Andrew Goodwin, eds. 1990. *On Record: Rock, Pop, and the Written Word*. New York: Pantheon.

Gardner, Howard. 1993. *Multiple Intelligences: The Theory in Practice*. New York: Basic Books.

Gaughan, John. 1997. *Cultural Reflections*. Portsmouth, NH: Heinemann.

Gitler, Ira. 1966. *Jazz Masters of the Forties*. New York: Collier.

Godwin, Gail. 1977. "Watcher at the Gate." *The New York Times*, 9 January, VII, 31.

Goldman, Albert. 1969. "It's Hard to Fake the True Blues: Johnny Winter." *Life* 67 (4 July): 8.

Gombrich, E. H., Julian Hochberg, and Max Black. 1972. *Art, Perception, and Reality*. Baltimore: Johns Hopkins University Press.

Goodwin, Andrew. 1990. "Sample and Hold: Pop Music in the Digital Age of Reproduction." In *On Record: Rock, Pop, and the Written Word*, edited by Simon Frith and Andrew Goodwin. New York: Pantheon.

Green, Jon D. 1990. "Determining Valid Interart Analogies." In *Teaching Literature and Other Arts*, edited by Jean-Pierre Barricelli, Joseph Gibaldi, Estella Lauter. New York: Modern Language Association.

Grossberg, Lawrence. 1992. *We Gotta Get Out of This Place*. New York: Routledge.

———. 1990. "Is There Rock After Punk?" In *On Record: Rock, Pop, and the Written Word*, edited by Simon Frith and Andrew Goodwin. New York: Pantheon.

"Guidelines for Educational Uses of Music." 1976. Reproduced in Circular 21, available from the U.S. Copyright Office, http://www.loc.gov/copyright.

Guralnick, Peter. 1990. "Eric Clapton at the Passion Threshold." *Musician* (February): 45–56.

Heins, Marjorie. 2002. "Screen Rage." *The Nation* 275 (4): 29–31.

Hennion, Antoine. 1990. "The Production of Success: An Antimusicology of the Pop Song." In *On Record: Rock, Pop, and the Written Word*, edited by Simon Frith and Andrew Goodwin. New York: Pantheon.

Hertsgaard, Mark. 1995. *A Day in the Life*. New York: Delacorte.

Hirsch, E. D. Jr., Joseph F. Kett, and James Trefil. 1988. *The Dictionary of Cultural Literacy: What Every American Needs to Know*. Boston: Houghton Mifflin.

Hodges, Donald A. 2000. "Implications of Music and Brain Research." *Music Education Journal* (September): 17–22.

Hornby, Nick. 1995. *High Fidelity*. New York: Riverhead.

Horton, Donald. [1957] 1990. "The Dialogue of Courtship in Popular Song." In *On Record: Rock, Pop, and the Written Word*, edited by Simon Frith and Andrew Goodwin. New York: Pantheon.

Hovland, Michael. 1986. *Musical Settings of American Poetry: A Bibliography*. New York: Greenwood.

Ice-T. 1997. *Musician* (February): 52.

Jameson, Frederick. 1984. "Postmodernism, or The Cultural Logic of Late Capitalism." *The New Left Review* 146: 53–92.

Jarrett, Michael. 1998. *Sound Tracks: A Musical ABC, Volumes 1–3*. Philadelphia: Temple University Press.

"John P. Saylor: Conservationist in Congress." Accessed 12/19/01: www.lib.iup.edu/spec_coll/exhibits/saylor/kinzaudam.html.

Kahn-Egan, Seth. 1998. "Pedagogy of the Pissed: Punk Pedagogy in the First-Year Writing Classroom." *College Composition and Communication* 49(1): 99–104.

Kelley, Tina. 2000. "Keats with a Guitar: The Times Sure Are A-Changin'." *The New York Times*, 9 January, 4–7.

Kim, Richard. 2001. "Eminem—Bad Rap?" *The Nation* (March 5): 4–5.

Kroeger, Fred. 1968. "A Freshman Paper Based on the Words of Popular Songs." *College Composition and Communication* 19 (5): 337–40.

Langer, Suzanne K. 1953. *Feeling and Form*. New York: Scribner's.

Lankewish, Vincent A. 1991. "Dramatic Monologue and Persona." In "Words and Music in the English Classroom." *English Journal* 80(8): 79.

Larsen, Cathy Allred. 2001. Personal e-mail to the author. 8 November.

Lawrence, John Shelton, and Bernard Timberg. 1989. *Fair Use and Free Inquiry*. 2d ed. Norwood, NJ: Ablex.

Lazere, Donald. 1994. "Teaching the Political Conflicts: A Rhetorical Schema." In *The Writing Teacher's Sourcebook*, 3d ed., edited by Gary Tate, Edward P. J. Corbett, and Nancy Myers. New York: Oxford University Press.

LeBlanc, Albert, Wendy L. Sims, Carolyn Sivola, Mary Obert. 1996. "Music Style Preferences of Different Age Listeners." *Journal of Research in Music Education* 44(1): 49–59.

Leland, John. 2001. "It's Only Rhyming Quatrains, But I Like It." *The New York Times Magazine*, 8 July, 36–39.

Leppert, Richard, and Susan McClary, eds. 1987. *Music and Society*. New York: Cambridge University Press.

Lester, Olivia. 2001. Personal e-mail to the author. 8 November.

Lora, Alice Chumbley. 1991. "From Reggae to Riddles." In "Words and Music in the English Classroom." *English Journal* 80 (8): 80.

Marcus, Greil. 1979. *Stranded: Rock and Roll for a Desert Island*. New York: Knopf.

Massey, Howard. 1999. "George Martin." *Musician* 243 (February): 30–42.

McLuhan, Marshall. 1964. *Understanding Media: The Extensions of Man*. New York: McGraw-Hill.

McNamee, Sheila. 2000. "Teaching as Conversation." Paper presented at American Psychological Association, Washington, DC, August.

McNeill, Lynne S. 2001. Personal e-mail to the author. 8 November.

Moody-Bouwhuis, Sherilynn. 2001. Personal e-mails to the author. 13, 14 November.

Murray, Donald M. 2001a. *The Craft of Revision.* 4th ed. Fort Worth, TX: Harcourt.

———. 2001b. *Write to Learn.* 7th ed. Boston: Heinle and Heinle.

———. 1983. "Write Badly to Write Well." Paper presented at Second Miami Conference on Sentence Combining and the Teaching of Writing, 21 October.

"Music and Politics." 1987. *Musician* (February): 61–62.

Negativland. 2001. "Shiny, Aluminum, Plastic, and Digital." Accessed 2/20/01 at www.negativland.com.

Newkirk, Thomas. 2002. "Sentimental Journeys: Anti-Romanticism and Academic Identity." *Writing with Elbow,* edited by Pat Belanoff, Marcia Dickson, Sheryl I. Fontaine, and Charles Moran. Logan: Utah State University Press.

O'Brien, Tim. 1990. *The Things They Carried.* New York: Penguin.

Obstfeld, Raymond, and Patricia Fitzgerald. 1997. *Jabberrock: The Ultimate Book of Rock 'n' Roll Quotations.* New York: Henry Holt.

Oehler, Paul. 1994. "I Sing the Body Electric: A Selected Discography of American Literature Set to Music." *Teaching English in the Two-Year College* 21 (December): 309–16.

———. 1998. "A Selected Discography of American Literature Set to Music Part II." *Teaching English in the Two-Year College* 21 (September): 25–28.

Ogdon, Bethany. 2001. "Review: Why Teach Popular Culture?" *College English* 63(4): 500–16.

Penha, James W. 1991. "Ears-on Experience of Prosody." In "Words and Music in the English Classroom." *English Journal* 80(8): 79.

Perry, William. 1970. *Forms of Intellectual and Ethical Development in the College Years.* New York: Holt.

Pirie, Bruce. 1997. *Reshaping High School English.* Urbana, IL: National Council of Teachers of English.

Pratt, Mary Louise. 1998. "Arts of the Contact Zone." In *Conversations in Context: Identity, Knowledge, and College Writing,* edited by Kathryn Fitzgerald, Heather Bruce, Sharon Stasney, and Anna Vogt. Fort Worth, TX: Harcourt.

Reed, Cheryl. 1997. "Technology, Popular Culture, and the Writing Classroom." *The Writing Instructor* (Spring): 99–102.

Reimer, Bennett. 1991. "Criteria for Quality in Music." In *Aesthetics and Arts Education,* edited by Ralph A. Smith and Alan Simpson. Urbana: University of Illinois Press.

Riesman, David. [1950] 1990. "Listening to Popular Music." In *On Record: Rock, Pop, and the Written Word,* edited by Simon Frith and Andrew Goodwin. New York: Pantheon.

Romano, Tom. 2000. *Blending Genre, Altering Style: Writing Multigenre Papers.* Portsmouth, NH: Boynton/Cook.

———. 1997. Foreword to *Cultural Reflections* by John Gaughan. Portsmouth, NH: Heinemann.

Rosenblatt, Louise. 1978. *The Reader the Text the Poem: The Transactional Theory of the Literary Work.* Carbondale: Southern Illinois University Press.

Sacks, Howard L., and Judith Rose Sacks. 1993. *Way Up North in Dixie: A Black Family's Claim to the Confederate Anthem.* Washington, DC: Smithsonian.

Santoro, Gene. 1993. "50 Foot Queenie." *The Nation* 256 (20): 715.

Schrank, Jeffrey. 1967. "Tribal Drums." *Media and Methods* (February): 29–31.

Shaughnessy, Mina. 1977. *Errors and Expectations.* New York: Oxford.

Shepherd, John. 1987. "Music and Male Hegemony." In *Music and Society,* edited by Richard Leppert and Susan McClary. Cambridge: Cambridge University Press.

Shusterman, Richard. 1991. "The Fine Art of Rap." *New Literary History* 22 (Summer): 613–32.

Sirc, Geoffrey. 1998. "Never Mind the Sex Pistols, Where's 2Pac?" *College Composition and Communication* 49(1): 104–108.

———. 1997. "Never Mind the Tagmemics, Where's the Sex Pistols?" *College Composition and Communication* 48(1): 9–29.

Spaethling, Robert. 1990. "Literature and Music." In *Teaching Literature and Other Arts,* edited by Jean-Pierre Barricelli, Joseph Gibaldi, Estella Lauter. New York: Modern Language Association.

Stambler, Irwin. 1977. *Encyclopedia of Pop, Rock, & Soul.* New York: St. Martin's.

Straw, Will. 1990. "Characterizing Rock Music Culture: The Case of Heavy Metal." In *On Record: Rock, Pop, and the Written Word,* edited by Simon Frith and Andrew Goodwin. New York: Pantheon.

Strong, William. 2001. *Coaching Writing: The Power of Guided Practice.* Portsmouth, NH: Heinemann.

Tannen, Deborah. 1990. *You Just Don't Understand: Men and Women in Conversation.* New York: Ballantine.

Tatum, Stephen. 1997. "The Problem of the 'Popular' in the New Western History." *Arizona Quarterly* 53(2): 153–90.

Temple, Johnny. 1999. "Noise from Underground: Punk Rock's Anarchic Rhythms Spur a New Generation to Political Activism." *The Nation* (18 Oct.): 17–22.

Thompson, G. R. 1973. *Poe's Fiction: Romantic Irony in the Gothic Tales.* Madison: University of Wisconsin Press.

Thompson, Stephen. 2001. Interview with Tom Lehrer. *The Onion A.V. Club.* Accessed 5/28/01: www.theavclub.com/avclub3619/avfeature_3619 .html.

Tipton, Juanita E. 1991. "The Horse before the Cart." In "Words and Music in the English Classroom." *English Journal* 80 (8): 77.

Tolkien, J. R. R. 1991 [1937]. *The Hobbit* and *The Lord of the Rings* boxed set. New York: Ballantine.

Toop, David. 1984. *The Rap Attack.* Boston: South End Press.

Van Der Meer, Tony. 1984. Introduction to *The Rap Attack.* Boston: South End Press.

Ventura, Michael. 1985. "Hear That Long Snake Moan." *Shadow Dancing in the USA.* Los Angeles: Tarcher.

Vygotsky, Lev S. 1962. *Thought and Language*. Cambridge, MA: MIT Press.

Waldron, Clarence. 1990. "Could Students Learn More If Taught with Rap Music?" *Jet* 77(16): 16–18.

Ward, Jennifer L. 2001. Personal e-mail to the author. 8 November.

Ward, Michael. 2001. Personal e-mail to the author. 14 November.

Watt, Ian. 1957. *The Rise of the Novel*. Berkeley: University of California Press.

Weathers, Winston. 1980. *An Alternate Style: Options in Composition*. Rochelle Park, NJ: Hayden.

Wener, Ben. 2000. "Morphine Soldiers on Without Mark Sandman." *The Orange County Register*, 31 January.

White, Edmund. 2001. "Before a Rendezvous with the Muse, First Select the Music." *New York Times*, 18 June, E1.

Whiteley, Sheila. 1997. "'The Sound of Silence': Academic Freedom and Copyright." *Popular Music* 16: 220–22.

Williams, Martin. 1983. *The Jazz Tradition*. New and revised ed. Oxford, England: Oxford University Press.

Willis, Paul. 1990. "The Golden Age." In *On Record: Rock, Pop, and the Written Word*, edited by Simon Frith and Andrew Goodwin. New York: Pantheon.

Wilson, Sondra Kathryn, ed. 1999. *In Search of Democracy*. New York: Oxford University Press.

"Words and Music in the English Classroom." 1991. *English Journal* 80 (8): 77–82.

Music

Allman Brothers Band, The. 1971. "Statesboro Blues." *Live at Fillmore East*. Polydor.

Amos, Tori. 1998. "Beulah Land." *Jackie's Strength*. Atlantic.

———. 1992. "Crucify," "Girl," "Happy Phantom," and "Precious Things." *Little Earthquakes*. Atlantic.

———. 1996. "Father Lucifer," "Hey Jupiter," "Muhammad My Friend," "Professional Widow," "Twinkle." *Boys for Pele*. Atlantic.

———. 1994. "God," "Icicle," and "Past the Mission." *Under the Pink*. Atlantic.

———. 1998. "iieee," "Pandora's Aquarium," and "Spark." *From the Choirgirl Hotel*. Atlantic.

———. 1994. "Sister Janet." *Cornflake Girl*. Atlantic.

———. 1992. "Smells Like Teen Spirit." *Crucify*. Atlantic.

Animals, The. 1964/1990. "House of the Rising Sun." *The Complete Animals*. EMI.

Arrested Development. 1992. "People Everyday." *3 Years, 5 Months and 2 Days in the Life of . . . .* Chrysalis.

Baez, Joan. 1970. "Joe Hill." *Woodstock*. Cotillion.

———. 1968. "Love Is Just a Four-Letter Word" (Dylan). *Any Day Now*. Vanguard.

Barbarians, The. 1966. "Are You a Boy or Are You a Girl?" *Are You a Boy or Are You a Girl?* One Way.

Beach Boys, The. 1965. "Help Me, Rhonda." *The Beach Boys Today!* Capitol.

———. 1964. "Johnny B. Goode." *The Beach Boys Concert.* Capitol.

Beastie Boys. 1986. "Fight for Your Right (to Party)." *Licensed to Ill.* Def Jam.

Beatles, The. 1995. "A Hard Day's Night." *The Beatles Anthology.* Apple.

———. 1964. "Ask Me Why." *Meet the Beatles.* Capitol.

———. 1969. "Because" and "I Want You (She's So Heavy)." *Abbey Road.* Apple.

———. 1966. "Eleanor Rigby." *Revolver.* Apple.

———. 1967. "The Fool on the Hill." *Magical Mystery Tour.* Parlophone.

———. 1967. "Good Morning Good Morning." *Sergeant Pepper's Lonely Hearts Club Band.* Capitol.

———. 1968. "Helter Skelter." *The Beatles.* Capitol.

———. 1965. "Nowhere Man." *Rubber Soul.* Capitol.

———. 1963. "Roll Over Beethoven." *With the Beatles.* Parlophone.

Beethoven, Ludwig van. 1823. *Symphony No. 9 in D Minor, Op. 125.*

Berry, Chuck. 1988. "Carol," "Johnny B. Goode," and "Roll Over Beethoven." *The Chess Box.* Chess.

Big Brother and the Holding Company. 1968. "Ball and Chain." *Cheap Thrills.* Columbia.

———. 1967/1993. "Roadblock." *Janis.* Columbia.

———. 1967. "Women Is Losers." *Big Brother and the Holding Company.* Columbia.

Brown, Greg. 1990. "If I Had Known." *Down in There.* Red House.

Brown, James. 1968/1996. "Say It Loud—I'm Black and I'm Proud." *Foundations of Funk: A Brand New Bag: 1964–1969.* Polydor.

Buffalo Springfield. 1967. "For What It's Worth." *Buffalo Springfield.* Atco.

Byrds, The. 1965/1992. "Mr. Tambourine Man." *The Byrds 20 Essential Tracks.* Columbia.

Captain Beefheart and His Magic Band. 1969. "Ant Man Bee," "The Blimp," and "Wild Life." *Trout Mask Replica.* Warner.

Clapton, Eric. 1992. "Layla." *Unplugged.* Reprise.

Cohan, George M. 1987. "Over There." *George M!* Sony.

Coltrane, John. 1964/1995. *A Love Supreme.* Impulse.

———. 1961/1972. "Chim Chim Cheree" and "Greensleeves." *The Best of John Coltrane: His Greatest Years Vol. 2.* ABC.

———. 1961/1987. "India." *Impressions.* Impulse.

———. 1961. "My Favorite Things." *My Favorite Things.* Atlantic.

Costello, Elvis. 1986. "I Want You." *Blood & Chocolate.* Columbia.

———. 1978. "No Action." *This Year's Model.* Rykodisc.

———. 1979. "(What's So Funny 'Bout) Peace, Love, and Understanding?" *Armed Forces.* Rykodisc.

Cream. 1968. "Crossroads" and "Pressed Rat and Warthog." *Wheels of Fire.* Polydor.

Crosby, Stills, Nash, and Young. 1970/1974. "Ohio." *So Far.* Atlantic.

Crystals, The. 1992. "He Hit Me (and It Felt Like a Kiss)" and "He's a Rebel." *The Best of the Crystals.* ABKCO.

Cure, The. 1989. "Disintegration." *Disintegration*. Elektra.

Dead Kennedys. 1980. "Kill the Poor." *Fresh Fruit for Rotting Vegetables*. Alternative Tentacles.

Dean, Jimmy. 1962/1995. "Big Bad John." *Greatest Songs*. Atlantic.

Derek and the Dominos. 1970. "Layla" and "Key to the Highway." *Layla & Other Assorted Love Songs*. Polydor.

Dethier, Brock. 1996. *Corey and Emma Are Found*. (Self-published song-and-story tape, available from the author.)

———. 1994. *Going to See the Doctor*. (Self-published song-and-story tape, available from the author.)

DiFranco, Ani. 1995. "Not a Pretty Girl." *Not a Pretty Girl*. Righteous Babe.

Doors, The. 1967. "Soul Kitchen." *The Doors*. Elektra.

Dylan, Bob. 1983/1991. "Blind Willie McTell." *Bob Dylan: The Bootleg Series*. Columbia.

———. 1994. "Hurricane." *Greatest Hits, Vol. 3*. Columbia.

———. 1975/1991. "Idiot Wind." *Blood on the Tracks* and *The Bootleg Series*. Columbia.

———. 1967. "I Dreamed I Saw St. Augustine." *John Wesley Harding*. Columbia.

———. 1966/1979. "I Want You." *Blonde on Blonde* and *At Budokan*. Columbia.

———. 1965/1970. "Like a Rolling Stone." *Highway 61 Revisited* and *Self Portrait*. Columbia.

———. 1964. "Lonesome Death of Hattie Carroll." *The Times They Are A-Changin'*. Columbia.

———. 1965. "Mr. Tambourine Man." *Bringing It All Back Home*. Columbia.

———. 1963. "Masters of War" and "Talkin' World War III Blues." *The Freewheelin' Bob Dylan*. Columbia.

———. 1969. *Nashville Skyline*. Columbia.

———. 1963/1991. "Talkin' John Birch Paranoid Blues." *The Bootleg Series*. Columbia.

———. 1966. "Visions of Johanna." *Blonde on Blonde*. Columbia.

Ellington, Duke. 1964/1994. "Take the 'A' Train." *The Great London Concerts*. Jazz Heritage.

Everly Brothers, The. 1960. "All I Have to Do Is Dream." *The Fabulous Style of the Everly Brothers*. Rhino.

Flack, Roberta. 1973. "Killing Me Softly with His Song." *Killing Me Softly*. Atlantic.

Franklin, Aretha. 1967/1986. "Respect." *30 Greatest Hits*. Atlantic.

Friend and Lover. 1968. "Reach Out of the Darkness." *Reach Out of the Darkness*. Verve.

Fugees (Refugee Camp). 1996. "Killing Me Softly with His Song" and "The Mask." *The Score*. Ruffhouse.

Garcia, Jerry, and Merl Saunders. 1988. "How Sweet It Is (To Be Loved by You)." *Keystone Encores, Vol. 1*. Fantasy.

Gaye, Marvin. 1964/1973/1983. "How Sweet It Is (To Be Loved by You)" and "Let's Get It On." *Marvin Gaye*. Tamla.

Grateful Dead, The. 1971/1987. "Johnny B. Goode." *The Grateful Dead*. Warner.

————. 1970. "New Speedway Boogie." *Workingman's Dead*. Warner.

————. 1981/1987. "Samson and Delilah." *Dead Set*. Arista.

Green Day. 1995. "Brat." *Insomniac*. Reprise.

Grisman, David. 1979. "Minor Swing." *Hot Dawg*. Horizon.

Handel, George Frederick. 1994. "Sonata in D Major, HWV371, Op. 1, No. 3." *Sonatas for Violin and Basso Continuo*. Denon.

Harvey, PJ. 1993. "Dry." *Rid of Me*. Island.

————. 1992. "Sheela-Na-Gig." *Dry*. Indigo.

Hendrix, Jimi. 2000. "Johnny B. Goode." *The Jimi Hendrix Experience* (Box Set). MCA.

————. 1967. "Little Wing." *Axis: Bold As Love*. Reprise.

————. 1970. "Star Spangled Banner." *Woodstock*. Cotillion.

Hill, Lauryn. 1998. "I Used to Love Him" and "When It Hurts So Bad." *The Miseducation of Lauryn Hill*. Ruffhouse.

Holiday, Billie. 2002. "Am I Blue." *Blue Billie*. Sony.

————. 1946/1991. "Strange Fruit" (Lewis Allan). *Billie Holiday Lady in Autumn*. Verve.

Hollies, The. 1969/1990. "He Ain't Heavy, He's My Brother." *Epic Anthology*. Epic.

————. 1964/1990. "Just One Look." *All Time Greatest Hits*. Curb.

Ian, Janis. 1967. "Society's Child." *Janis Ian*. Verve.

Insect Trust. 1968. "Declaration of Independence." *Insect Trust*. Capitol.

Jefferson Airplane. 1971. "Pretty as You Feel." *Bark*. RCA.

————. 1967. "A Small Package of Value Will Come to You, Shortly." *After Bathing at Baxter's*. RCA.

Johnny Kidd and the Pirates. 1960/1994. "Shakin' All Over." *Complete Johnny Kidd*. EMI.

Johnson, Robert. 1936/1990. "Cross Road Blues." *The Complete Recordings*. Columbia.

Joplin, Janis. 1962/1993. "What Good Can Drinkin' Do." *Janis*. Columbia.

Judas Priest. 1988. "Johnny B. Goode." *Ram It Down*. Columbia.

Lee, Dickey. 1962. "Patches." *The Tale of Patches*. Smash.

Lehrer, Tom. 1965. "New Math," "Pollution," "Who's Next." *That Was the Year That Was*. Reprise.

————. 1959/1966. "Oedipus Rex" and "We Will All Go Together When We Go." *An Evening Wasted with Tom Lehrer*. Reprise.

Lennon, John. 1975. "Cold Turkey." *Shaved Fish*. Capitol.

————. 1970. "God." *Plastic Ono Band*. Capitol.

Loggins, Kenny, and Jim Messina. 1976. "Danny's Song." *The Best of Friends*. Columbia.

Lomax, Alan. 1999. *Negro Work Songs & Calls*. Rounder.

Madonna. 1990. "Papa Don't Preach." Video. *Madonna—the Immaculate Collection*. Warner.

Mahal, Taj. 1969/1989. "Linin' Track." *Giant Step*. Columbia.

Malmsteen, Yngwie. 1984. *Rising Force*. Mercury.

Marley, Bob, and the Wailers. 1984. "One Love/People Get Ready." *Legend*. Island.

McFerrin, Bobby. 1988. "Don't Worry, Be Happy." *Don't Worry, Be Happy*. EMI.

Minor Threat. 1981/1983/1989. "In My Eyes." *Complete Discography*. Dischord.

Mitchell, Joni. 1970. "Big Yellow Taxi." *Ladies of the Canyon*. Reprise.

———. 1969. "Both Sides Now." *Clouds*. Reprise.

Morphine. 1993. *Cure for Pain*. Rykodisc.

Near, Holly, and Ronnie Gilbert. 1983. "Biko." *Lifeline*. Redwood.

Nine Inch Nails. 1989. "Sanctified." *Pretty Hate Machine*. TVT.

Nirvana. 1993. "All Apologies" and "Radio Friendly Unit Shifter." *In Utero*. DGC.

———. 1989. "Love Buzz." *Bleach*. Sub Pop.

———. 1991. "Smells Like Teen Spirit" and "Territorial Pissings." *Nevermind*. DGC.

Orlando, Tony, and Dawn. 1973/1999. "Tie a Yellow Ribbon 'Round the Ole Oak Tree." *Knock Three Times*. BMG.

Oscar Peterson–Stephane Grappelli Quartet. 1973. "Them There Eyes." *Oscar Peterson–Stephane Grappelli Quartet*. America.

Parker, Charlie, and Dizzy Gillespie. 1950/1997. "Leap Frog." *Bird and Diz*. Verve.

Peter, Paul, and Mary. 1962. "If I Had My Way." *Peter Paul and Mary*. Warner.

Phair, Liz. 1993. *Exile in Guyville*. Matador.

Phish. 1998. "Guyute." *Story of the Ghost*. Elektra.

Pink Floyd. 1979. "Another Brick in the Wall, Part 2." *The Wall*. Columbia.

Poco. 1971. "You'd Better Think Twice." *Deliverin*. Epic.

Prine, John. 1971. "Hello in There." *John Prine*. Atlantic.

Procol Harum. 1967. "A Whiter Shade of Pale." *Procol Harum*. Deram.

Public Enemy. 1988. "Party for Your Right to Fight." *It Takes a Nation of Millions to Hold Us Back*. Def Jam.

Quicksilver Messenger Service. 1970. "Fresh Air." *Just for Love*. One Way.

———. 1970. "What About Me." *What About Me*. One Way.

Rage Against the Machine. 1999. *The Battle of Los Angeles*. Epic.

Ramones, The. 1978. "I Wanna Be Sedated." *Road to Ruin*. Sire.

Replacements, The. 1987. "The Ledge." *Pleased to Meet Me*. Sire.

Rolling Stones, The. 1970. "Carol." *Get Yer Ya-Ya's Out*. ABKCO.

———. 1965. "Satisfaction." *Out of Our Heads*. ABKCO.

———. 1968. "Sympathy for the Devil." *Beggars Banquet*. ABKCO.

———. 1966. "Under My Thumb" and "Stupid Girl." *Aftermath*. ABKCO.

Sainte-Marie, Buffy. 1966/1964/1987. "My Country 'Tis of Thy People You're Dying" and "Now That the Buffalo's Gone." *The Best of Buffy Sainte-Marie*. Vanguard.

Santana. 1999. *Supernatural*. Arista.

Seeger, Peggy. 1971/1998. "I'm Gonna Be an Engineer." *Period Pieces*. Tradition.

Sex Pistols, The. 1977. "God Save the Queen." *Never Mind the Bollocks Here's the Sex Pistols*. Warner.

Simon & Garfunkel. 1966. "The Dangling Conversation." *Parsley, Sage, Rosemary & Thyme*. Columbia.

————. 1966. "I Am a Rock." *The Sounds of Silence*. Columbia.

Sinkhole. 1995. "Fudge Bar." *Space Freak*. Ringing Ear.

Sleater-Kinney. 1999. "Burn, Don't Freeze" and "God Is a Number." *The Hot Rock*. Kill Rock Stars.

————. 1997. "Not What You Want." *Dig Me Out*. Kill Rock Stars.

Sly and the Family Stone. 1969. "Everyday People." *Stand*. Epic.

Smith, Patti. 1978. "Babelogue" and "Ghost Dance." *Easter*. Arista.

————. 1975. "Gloria." *Horses*. Arista.

Smiths, The. 1986. "Cemetry Gates." *The Queen Is Dead*. Sire.

Sommers, Joanie. 1962. "Johnny Get Angry." *Johnny Get Angry*. Warner.

Spears, Britney. 2000. "Oops! ... I Did It Again." *Oops!...I Did It Again*. BMG.

Spirit. 1970. "Nature's Way." *The Twelve Dreams of Dr. Sardonicus*. Epic.

Springsteen, Bruce. 1984. "Born in the USA." *Born in the USA*. Columbia.

Talking Heads. 1983. "This Must Be the Place (Naive Melody)." *Speaking in Tongues*. Sire.

Them. 1964/1987. "Gloria" (Van Morrison). *Them*. London.

Vega, Suzanne. 1987. "Luka." *Solitude Standing*. A&M.

Velvet Underground, The. 1967. "Heroin." *The Velvet Underground & Nico*. Verve.

West Coast Pop Art Experimental Band. 1969/2001. "A Child of a Few Hours Is Burning to Death." *Volume III: A Child's Guide to Good and Evil*. Sundazed.

Who, The. 1969. *Tommy*. MCA.

Williams, Hank. 1949/1978. "I'm So Lonesome I Could Cry." *Hank Williams: 40 Greatest Hits*. Polydor.

Winter, Johnny. 1971. "Johnny B. Goode." *Johnny Winter and . . . Live*. Columbia.

X. 1980. "Soul Kitchen" and "The World's a Mess, It's in My Kiss." *Los Angeles*. Slash.

————. 1981. *Wild Gift*. Slash.

Yes. 1972. "Siberian Khatru." *Close to the Edge*. Atlantic.

Young, Neil. 1970. "After the Gold Rush." *After the Gold Rush*. Reprise.

————. 1975. "Cortez the Killer." *Zuma*. Reprise.

————. 1969. "Down by the River." *Everybody Knows This Is Nowhere*. Reprise.

————. 1979. "My My, Hey Hey (Out of the Blue)." *Rust Never Sleeps*. Reprise.

Youngbloods. 1967. "Get Together." *The Youngbloods*. Edsel.

Zappa, Frank, and the Mothers of Invention. 1968. "Stuff Up the Cracks." *Cruising with Ruben and the Jets*. Rykodisc.

Zwilich, Ellen Taaffe. 1989. "Concerto Grosso 1985." *Ellen Taaffe Zwilich*. New World Records.

Index

Note: Most songs and albums are indexed only under the performer's name.